Animal Adult Coloring Book

I0513954

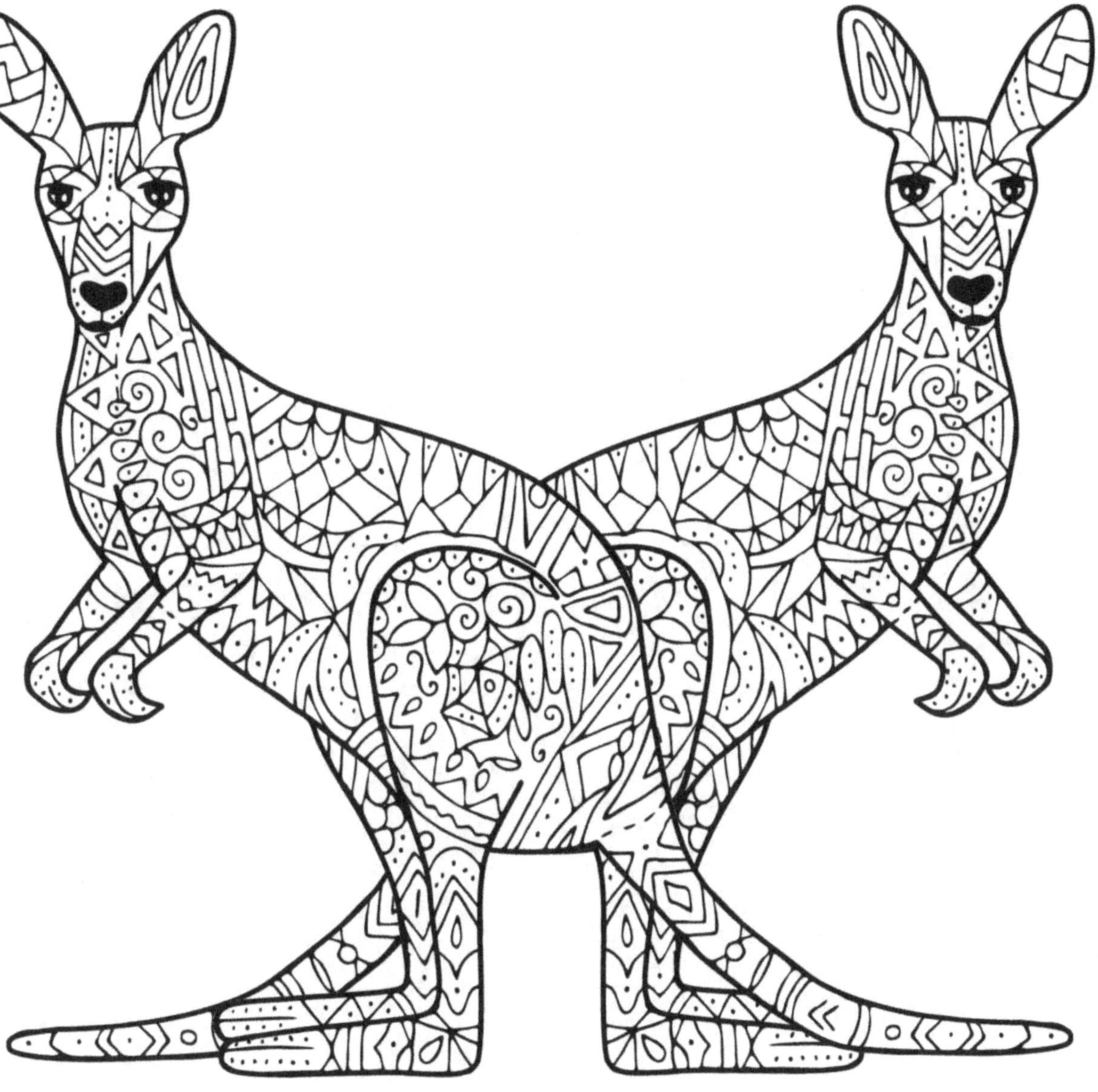

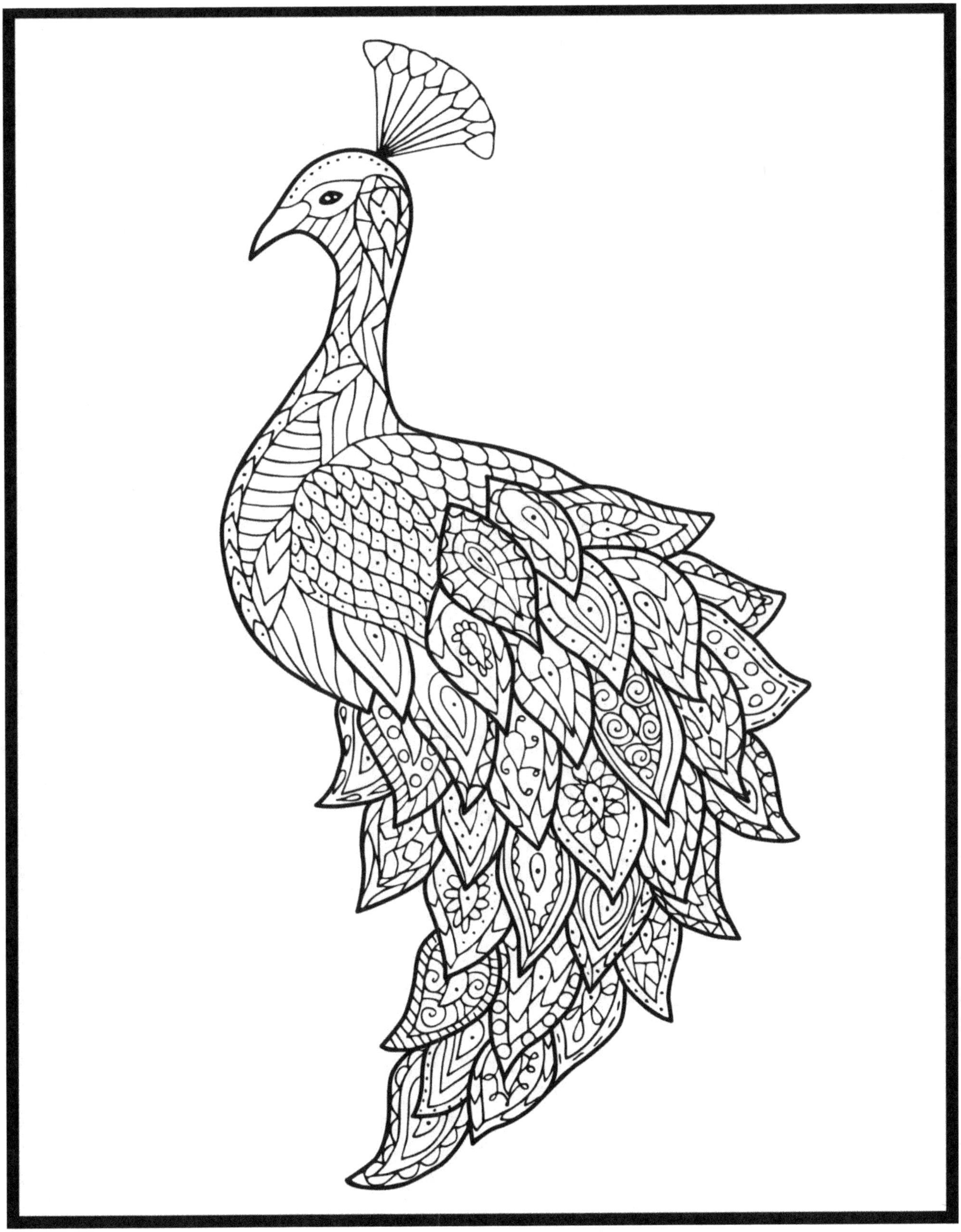

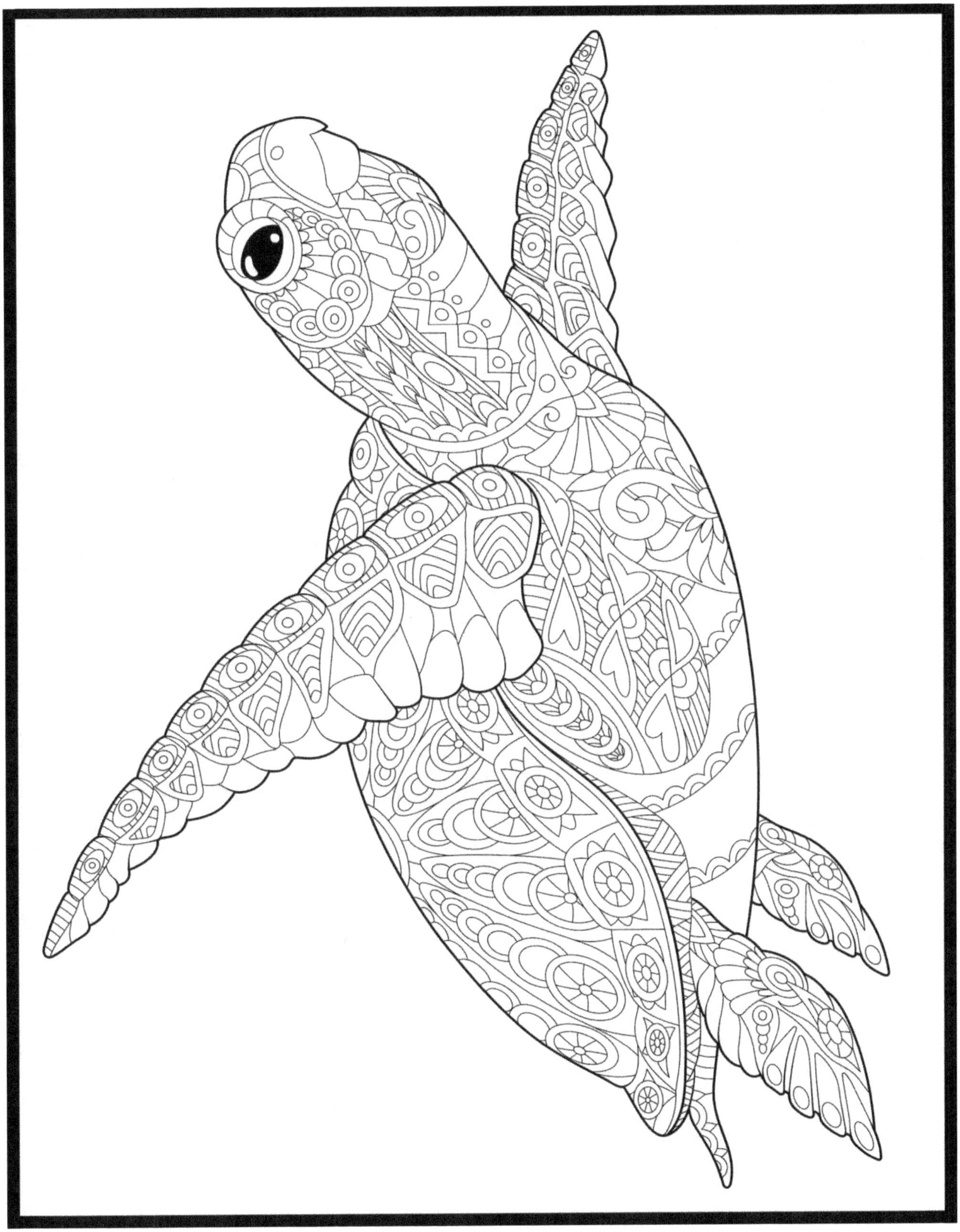

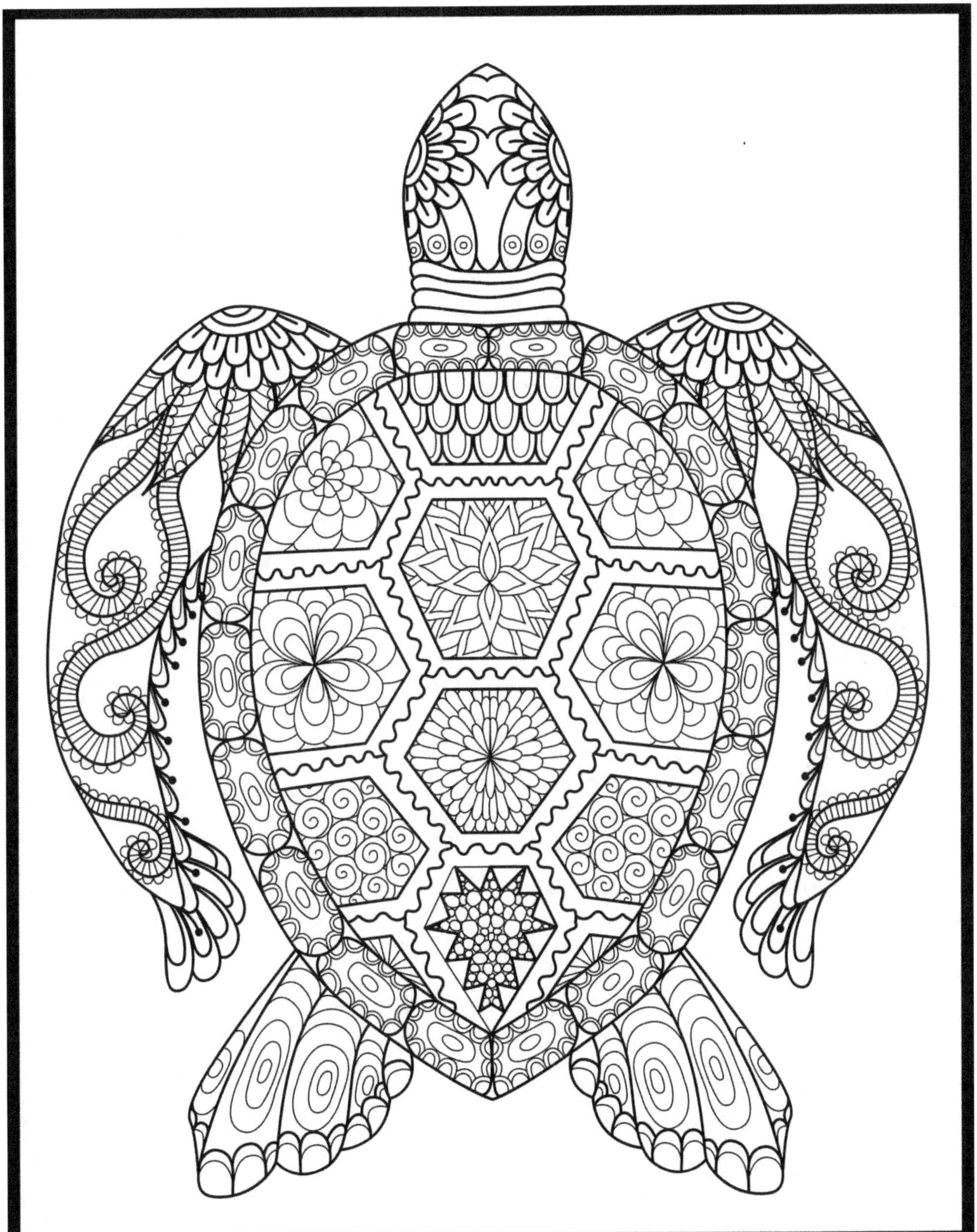

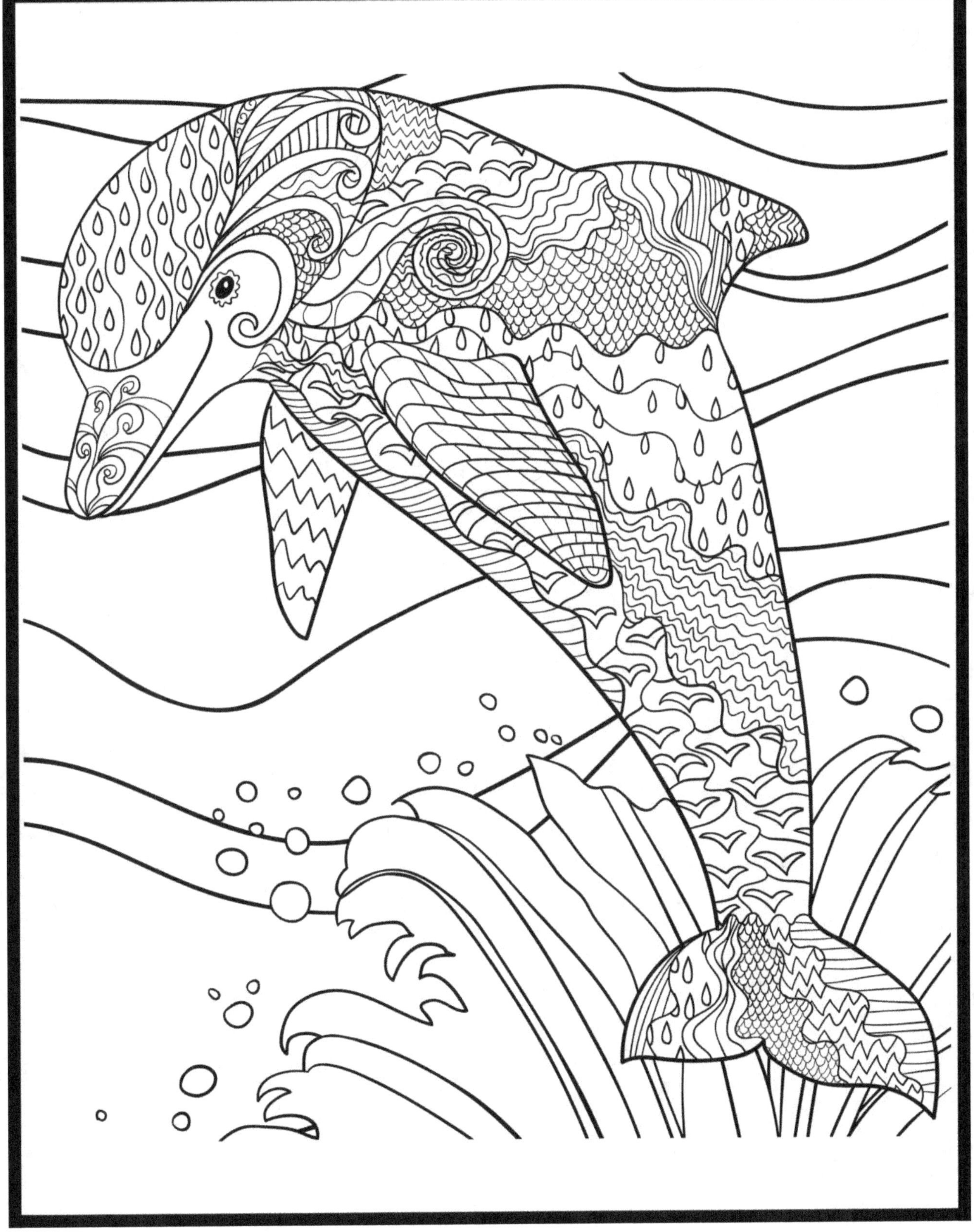

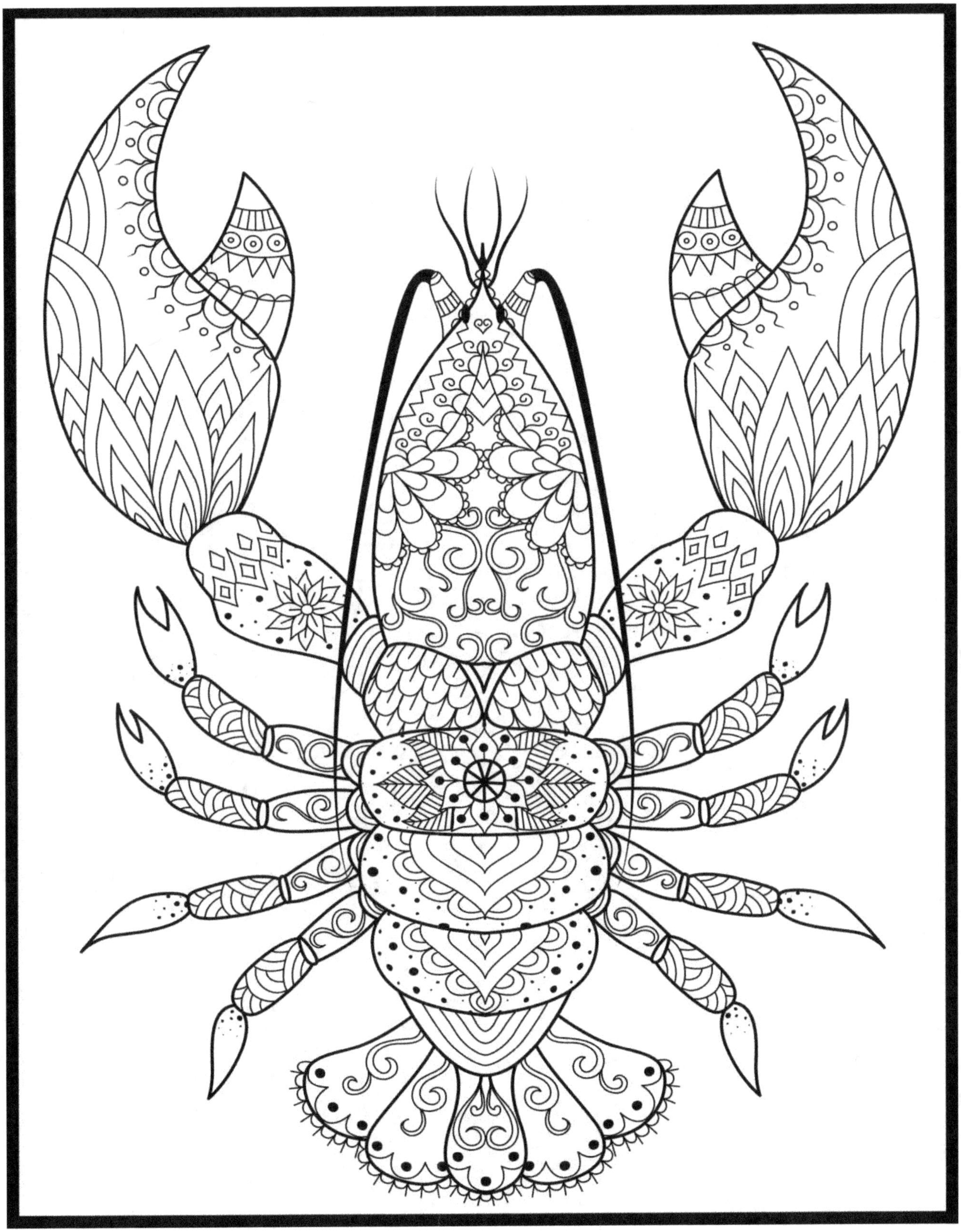

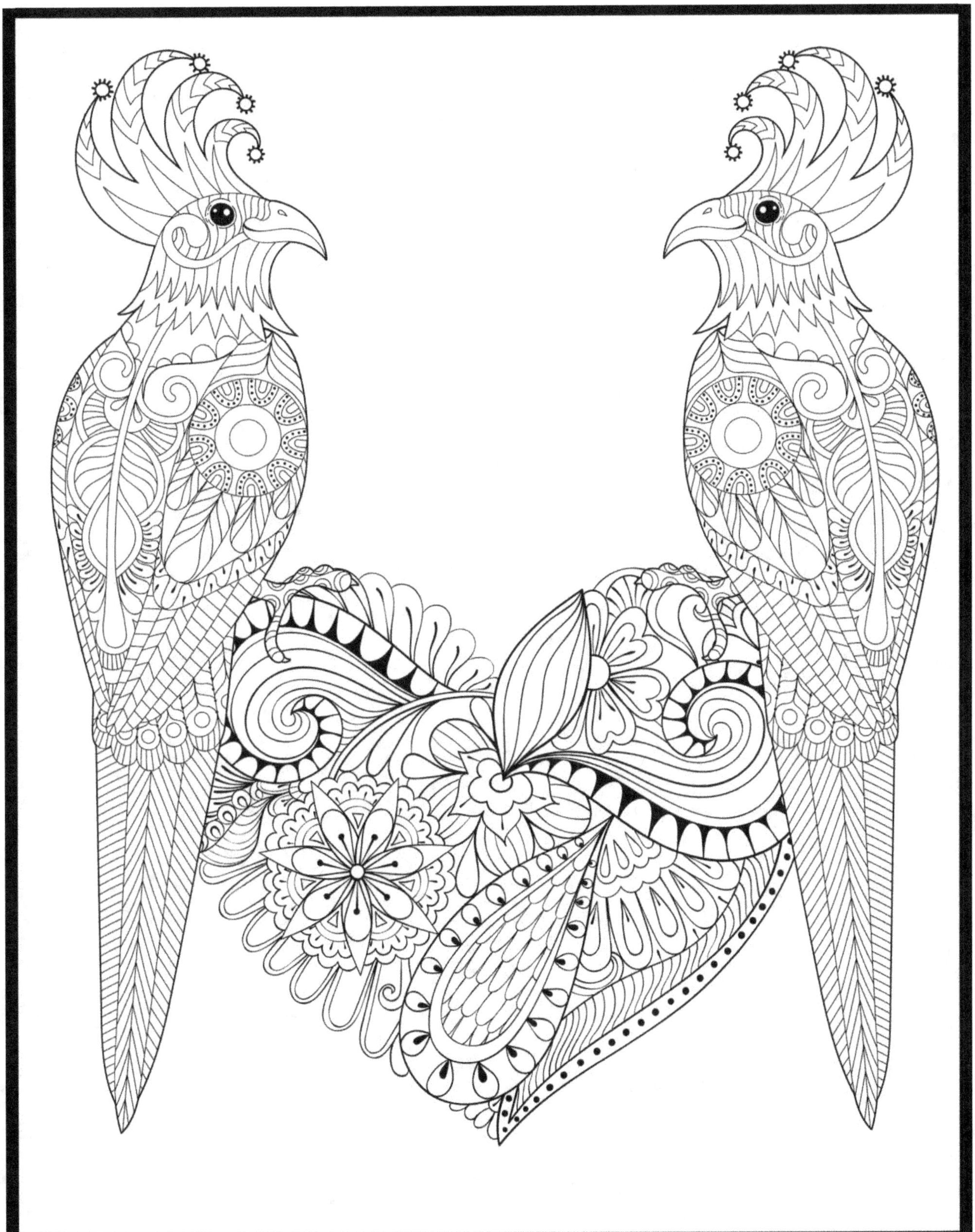

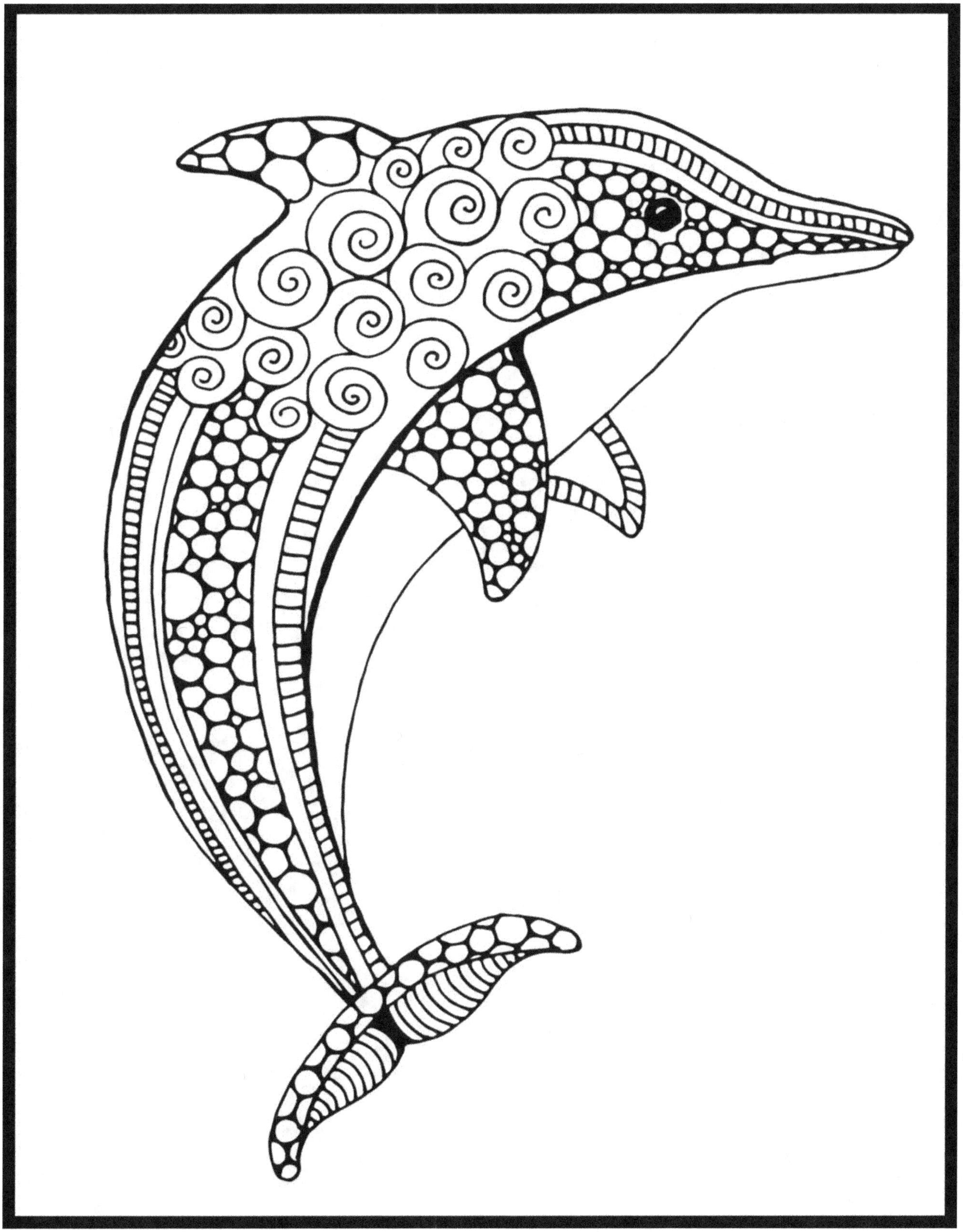

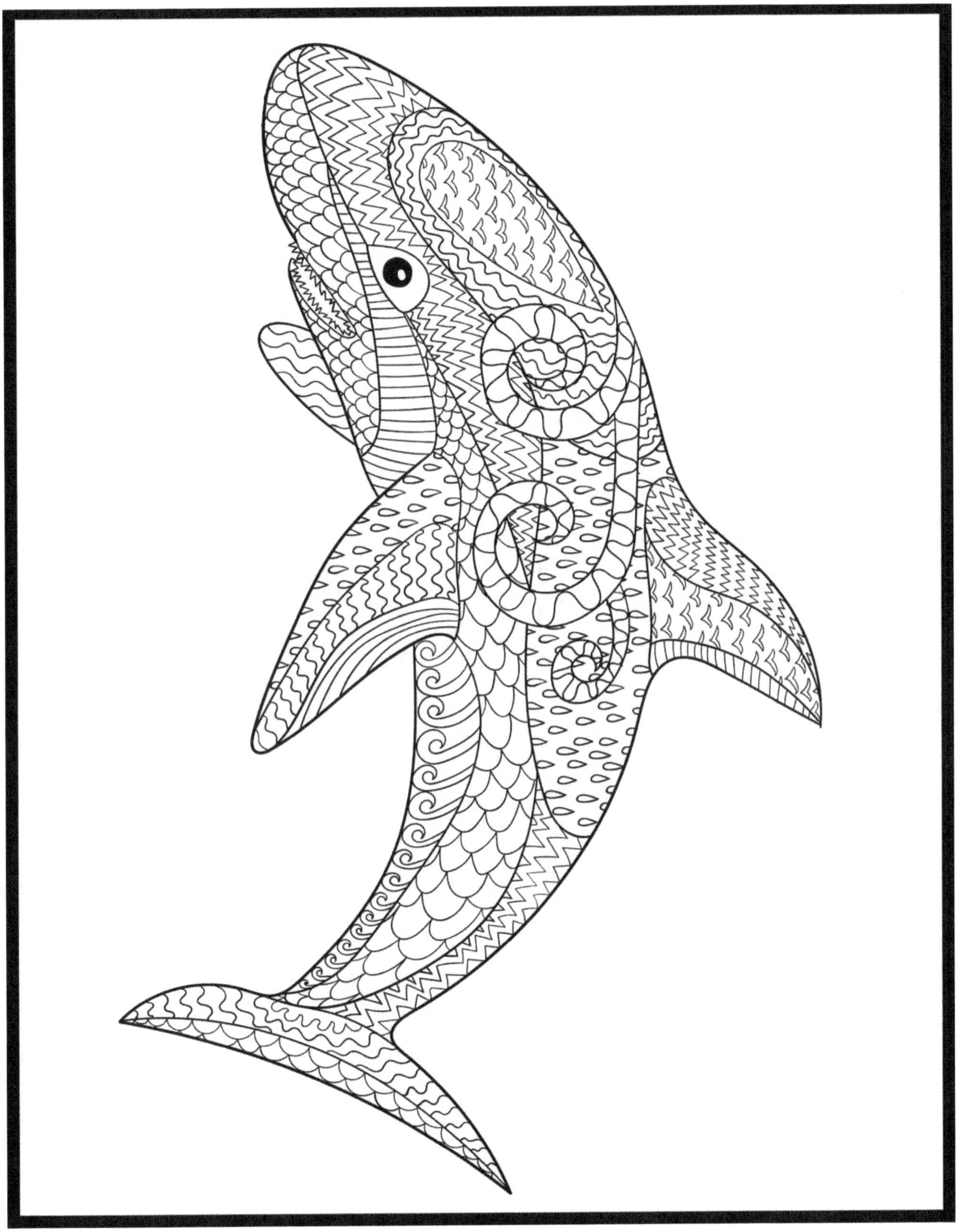

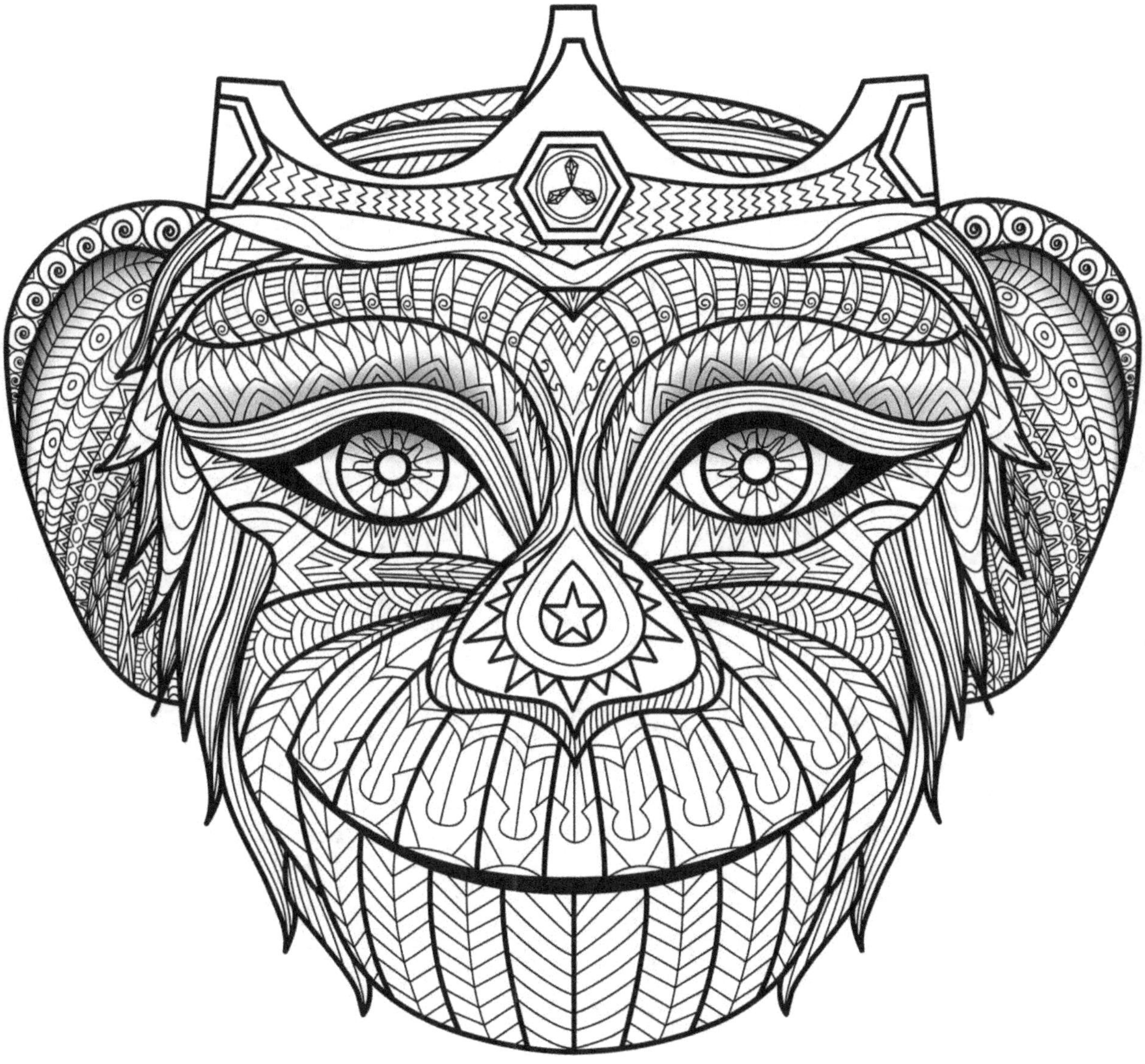

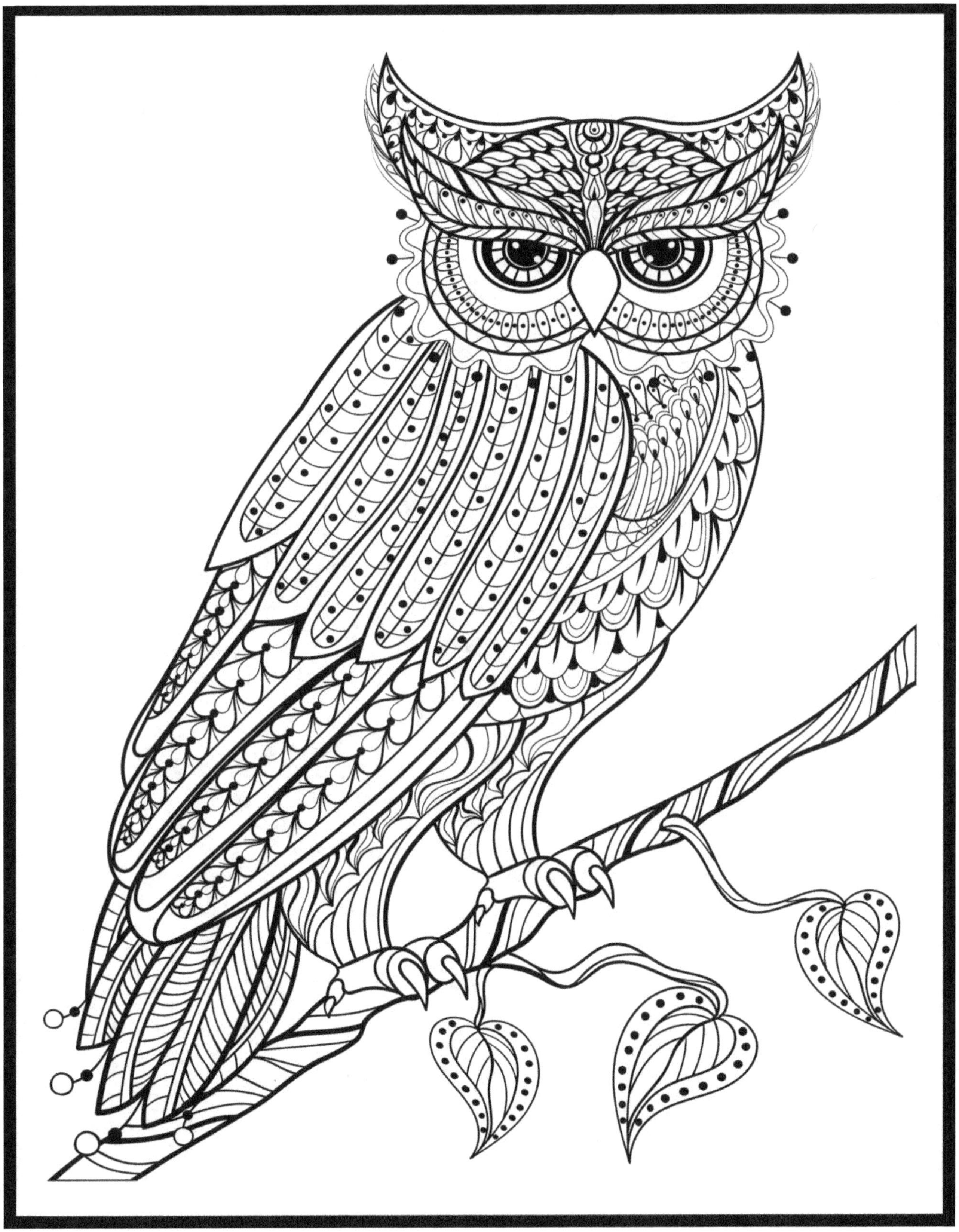

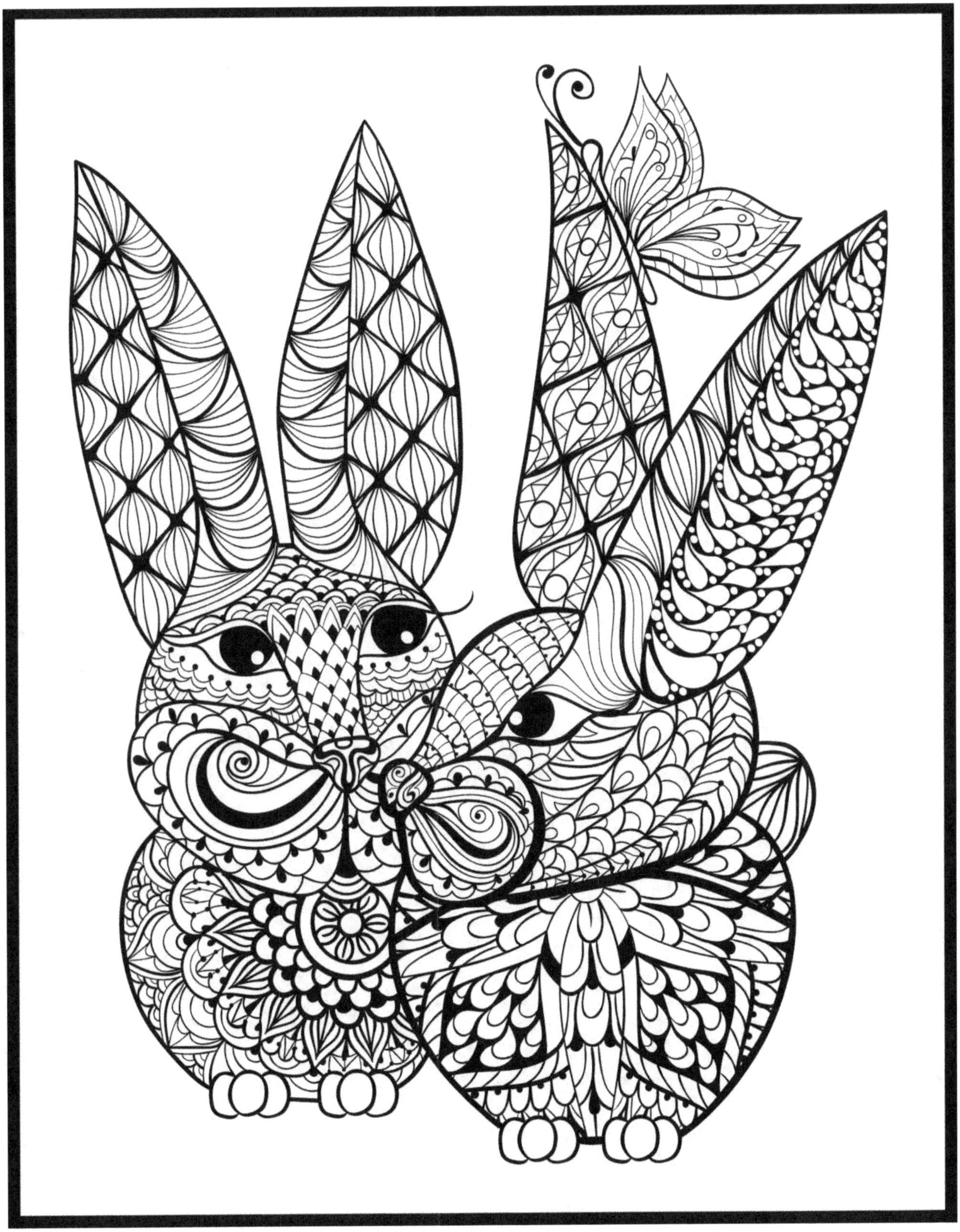

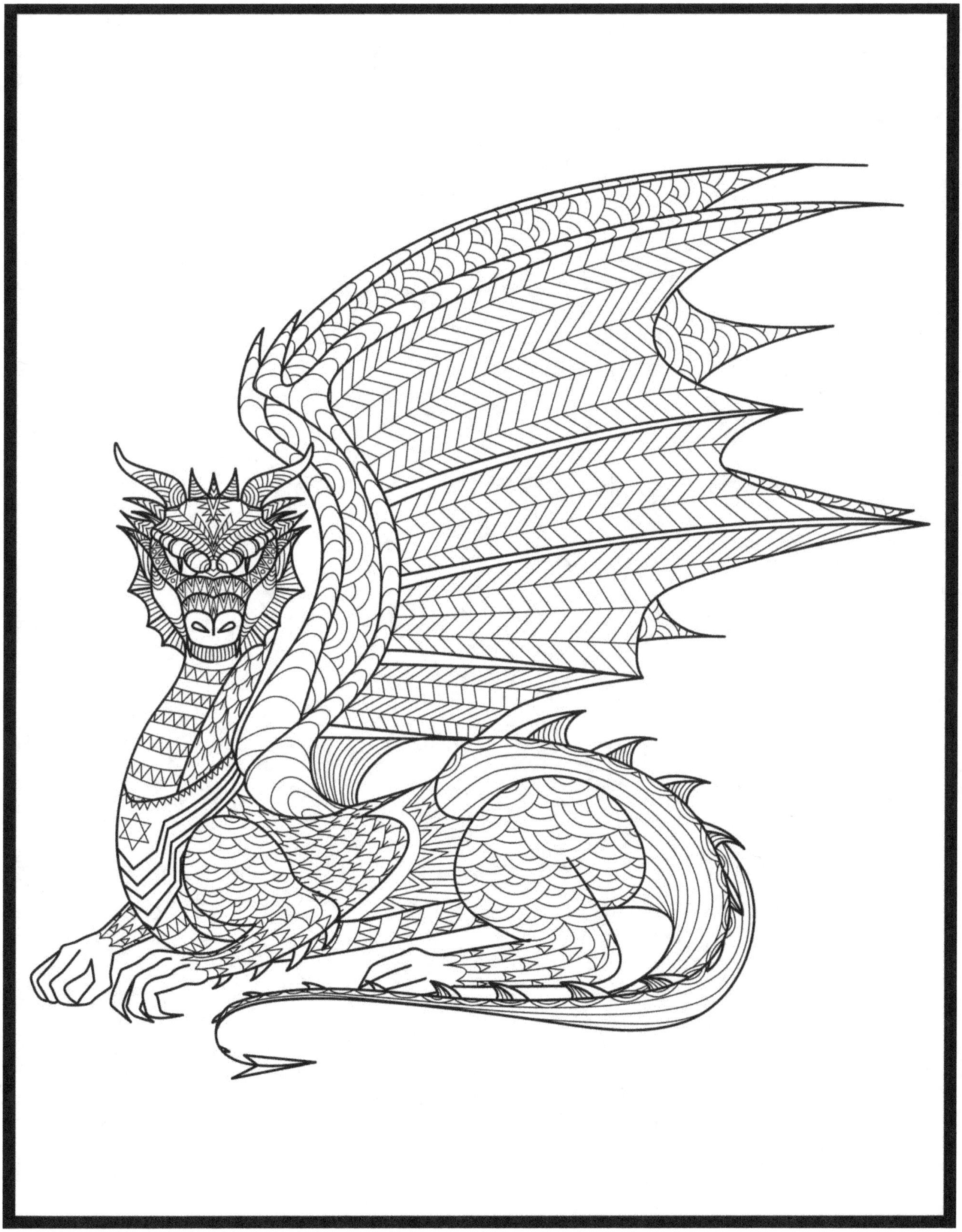

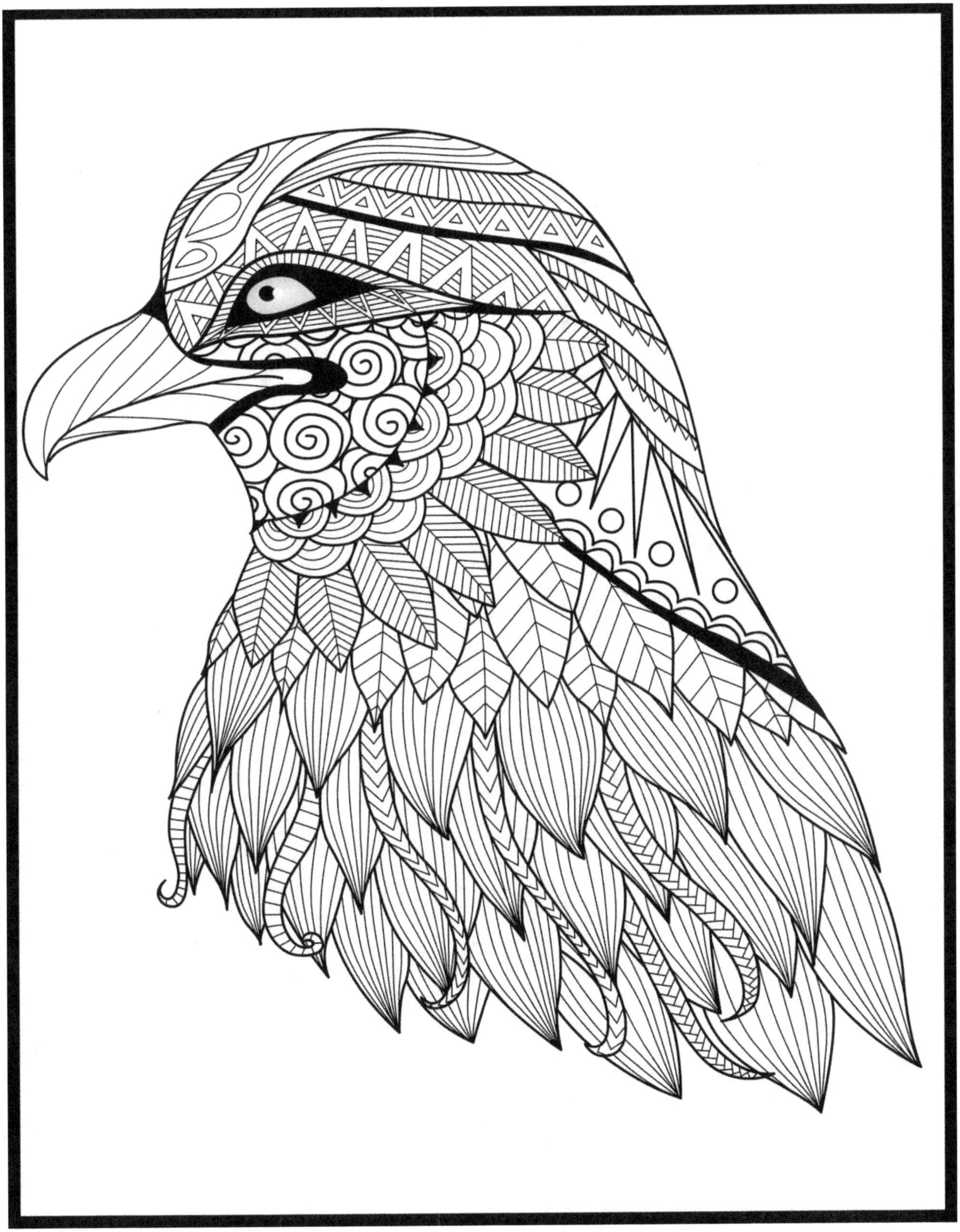

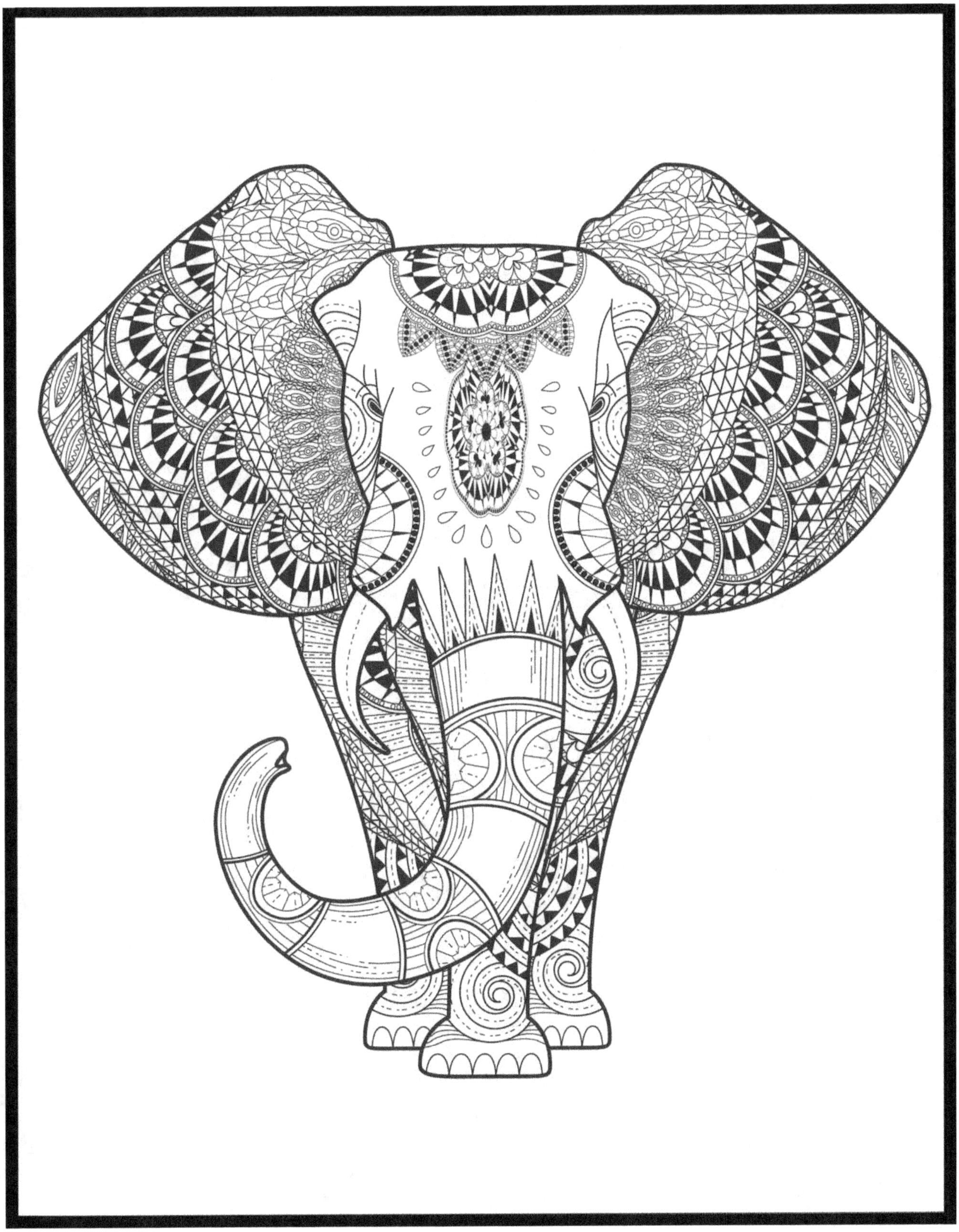

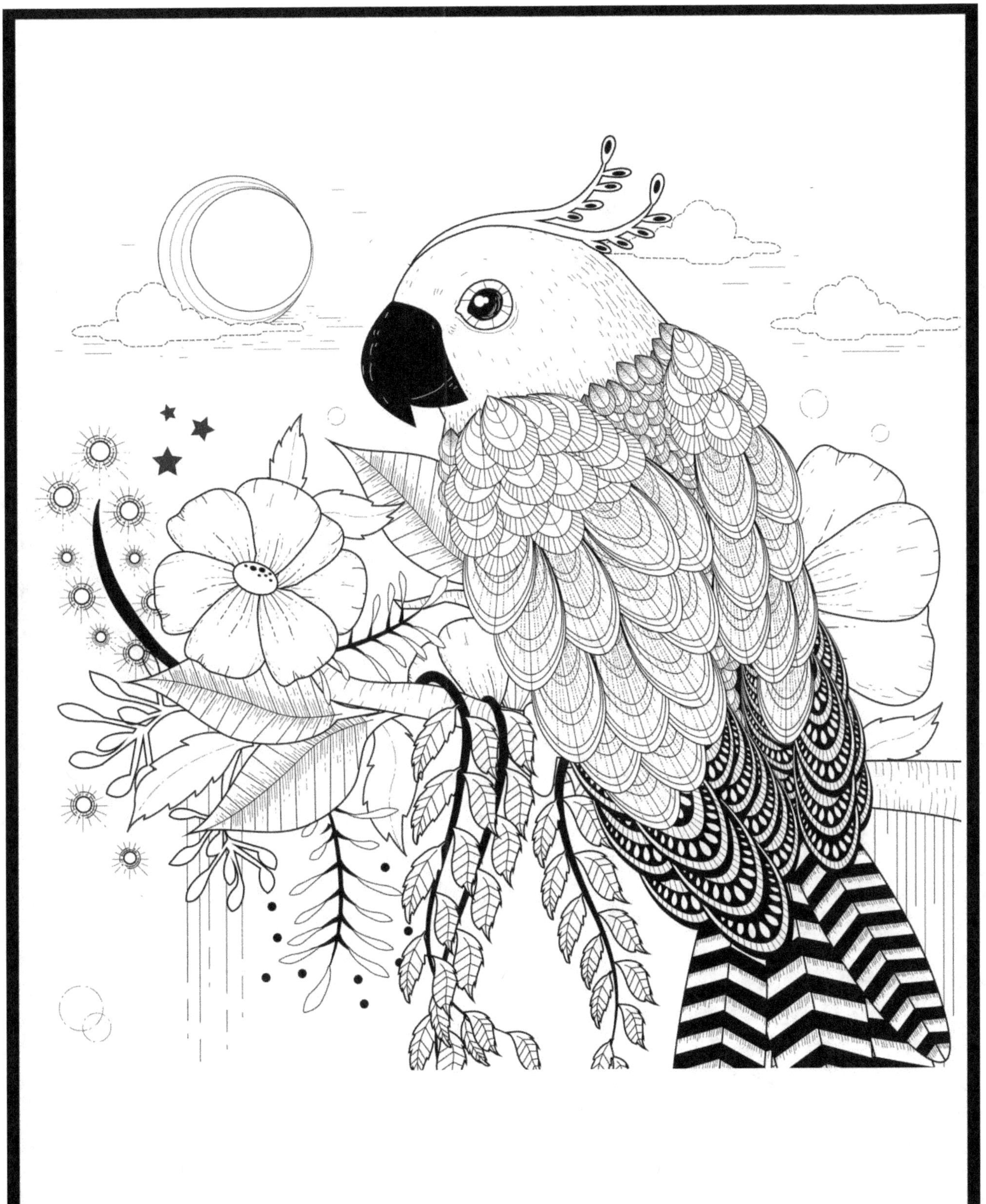

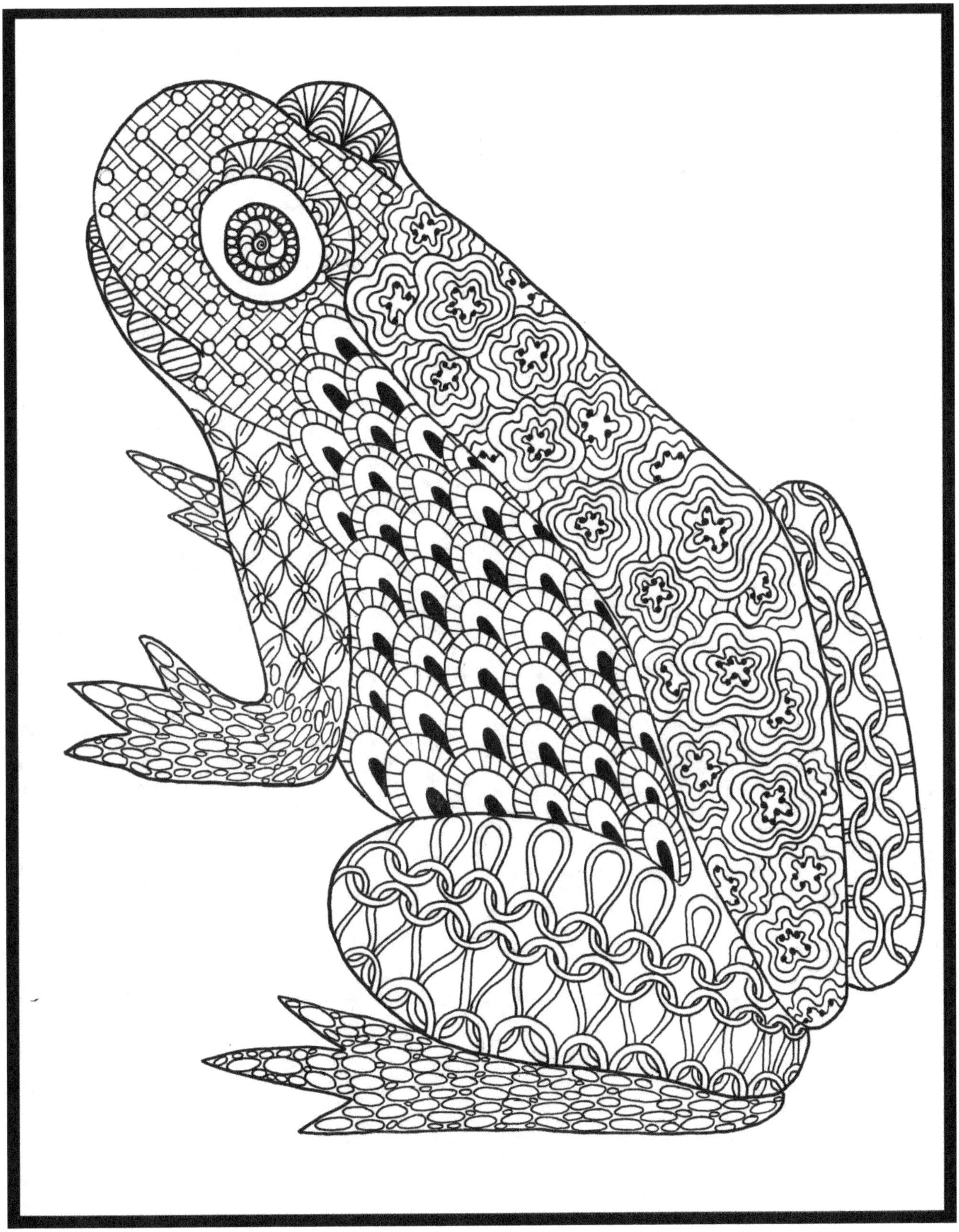

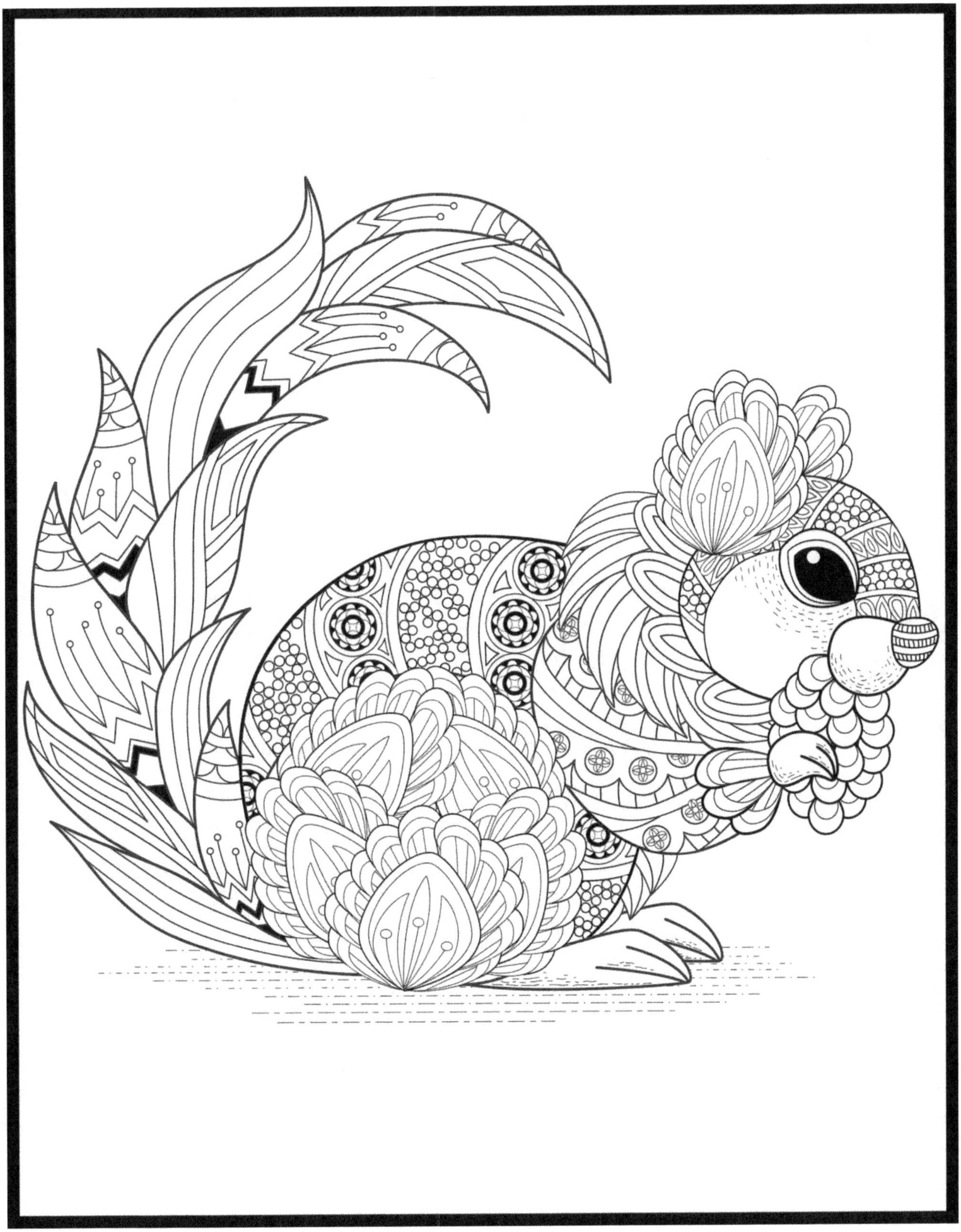

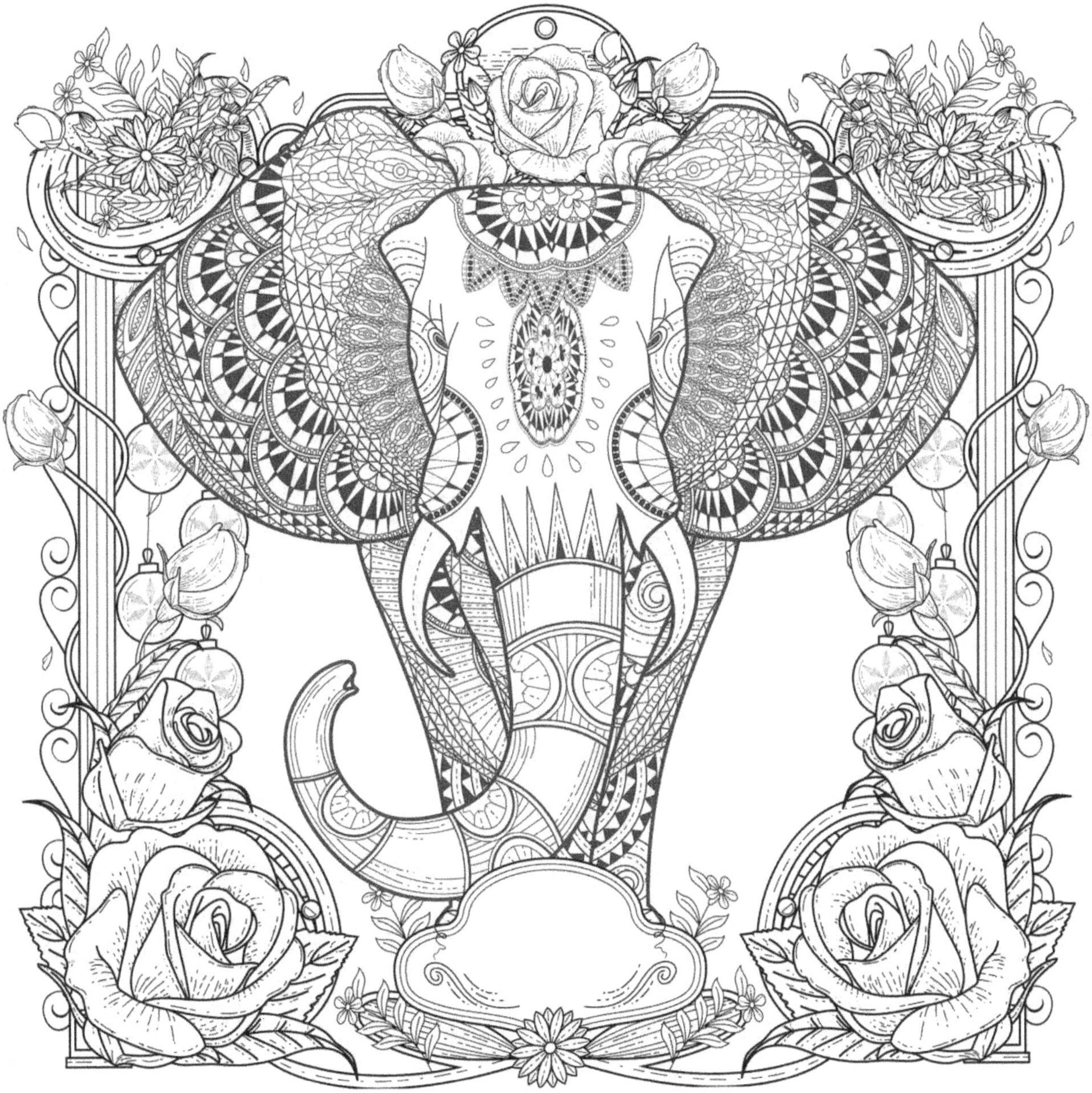

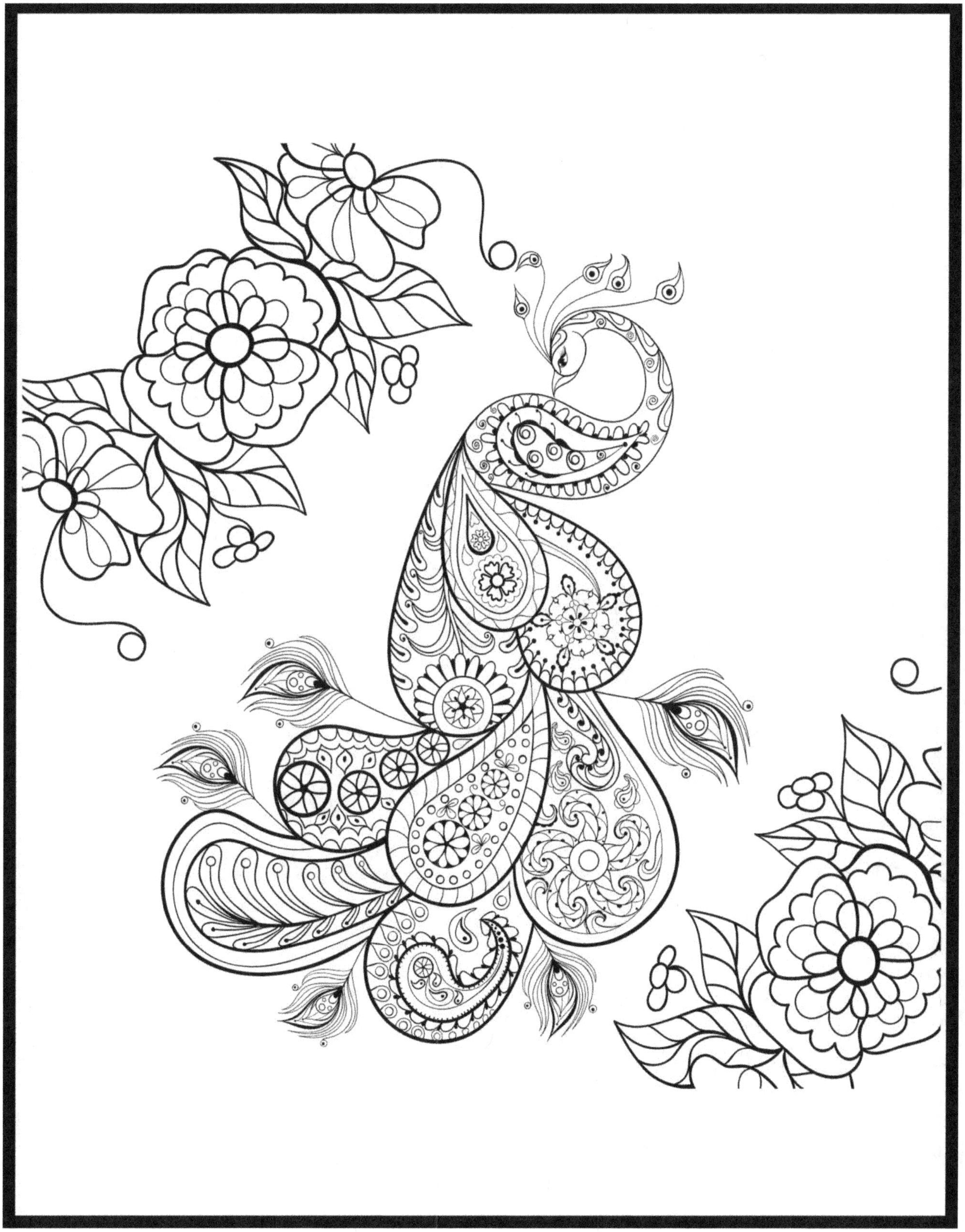

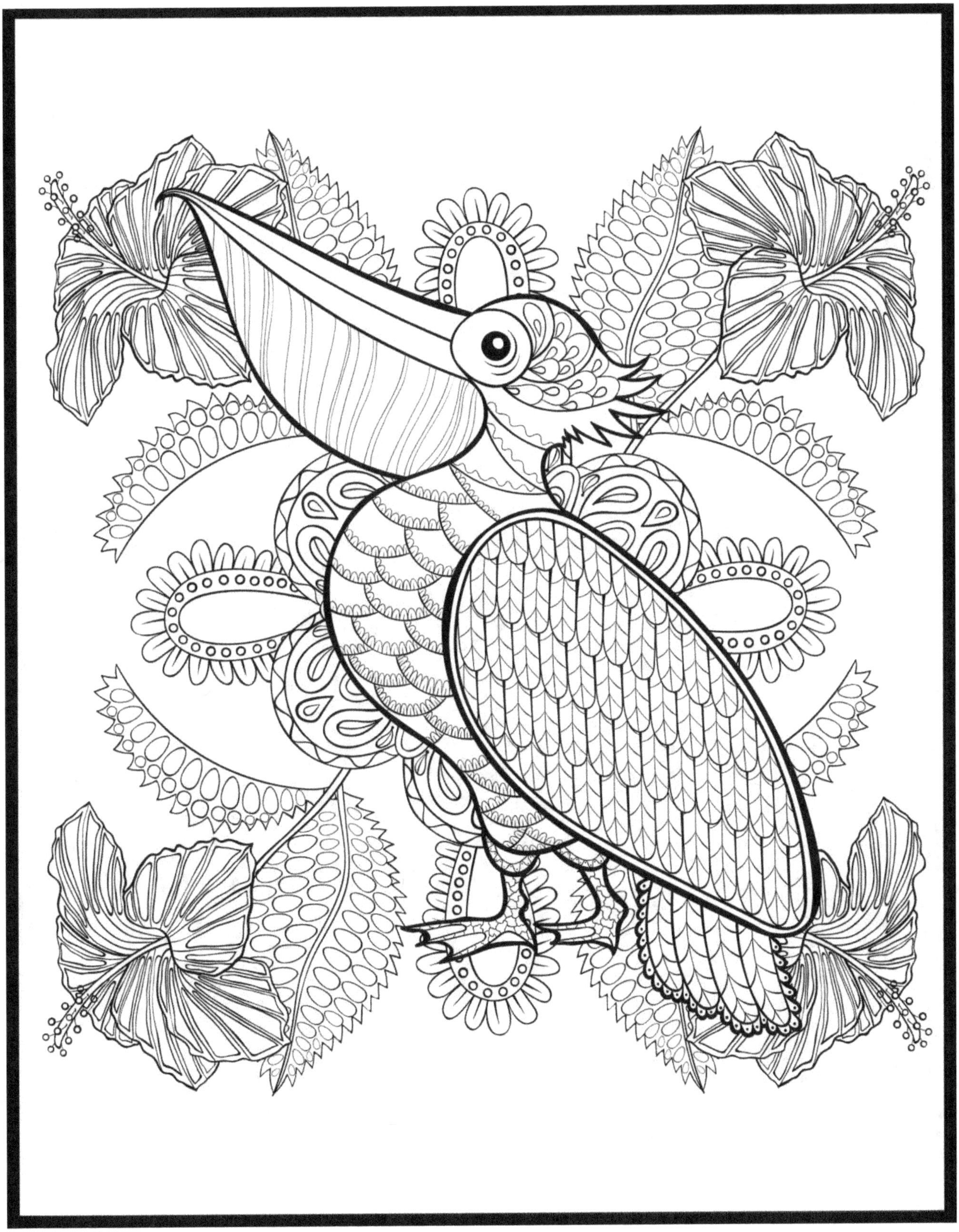

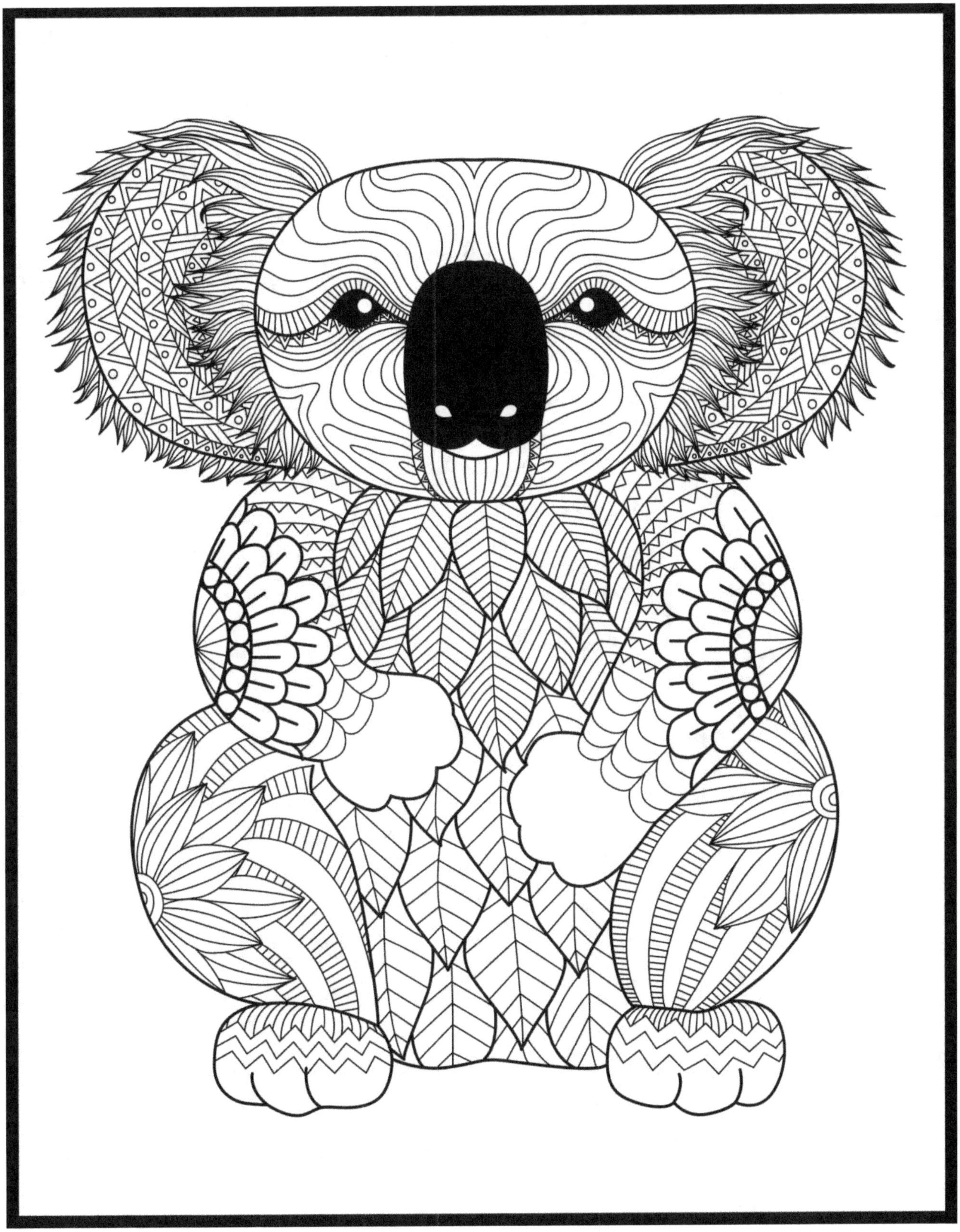

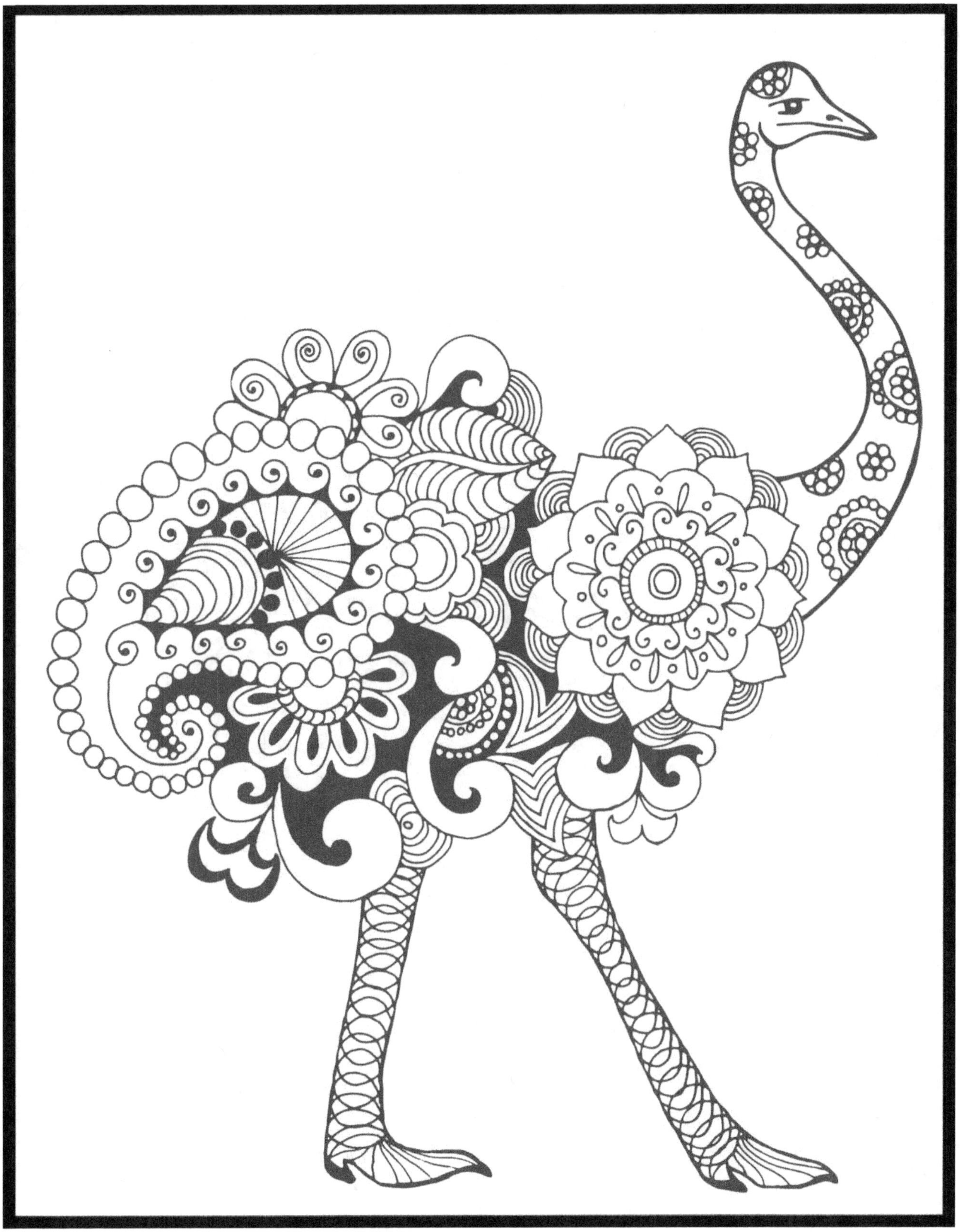

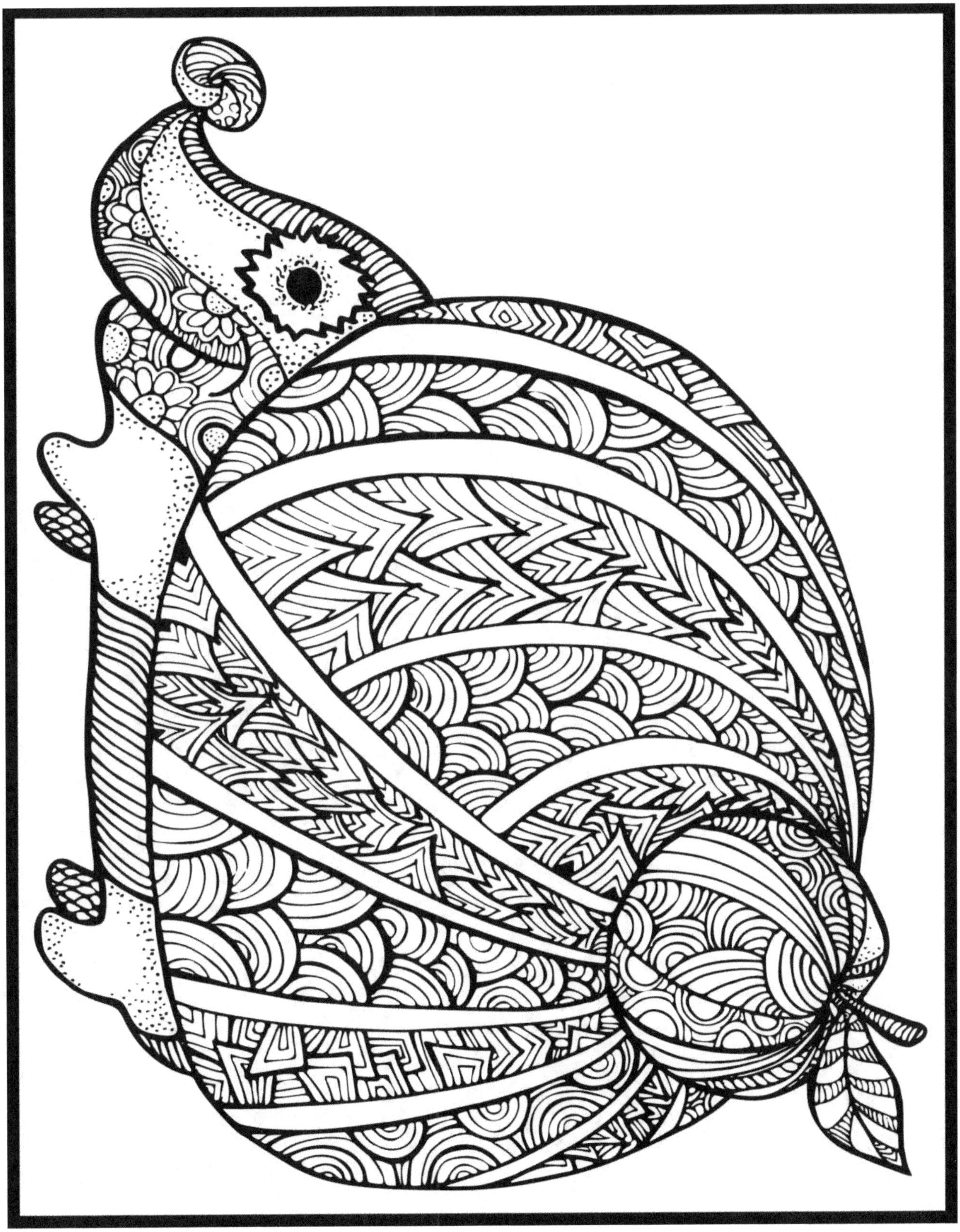

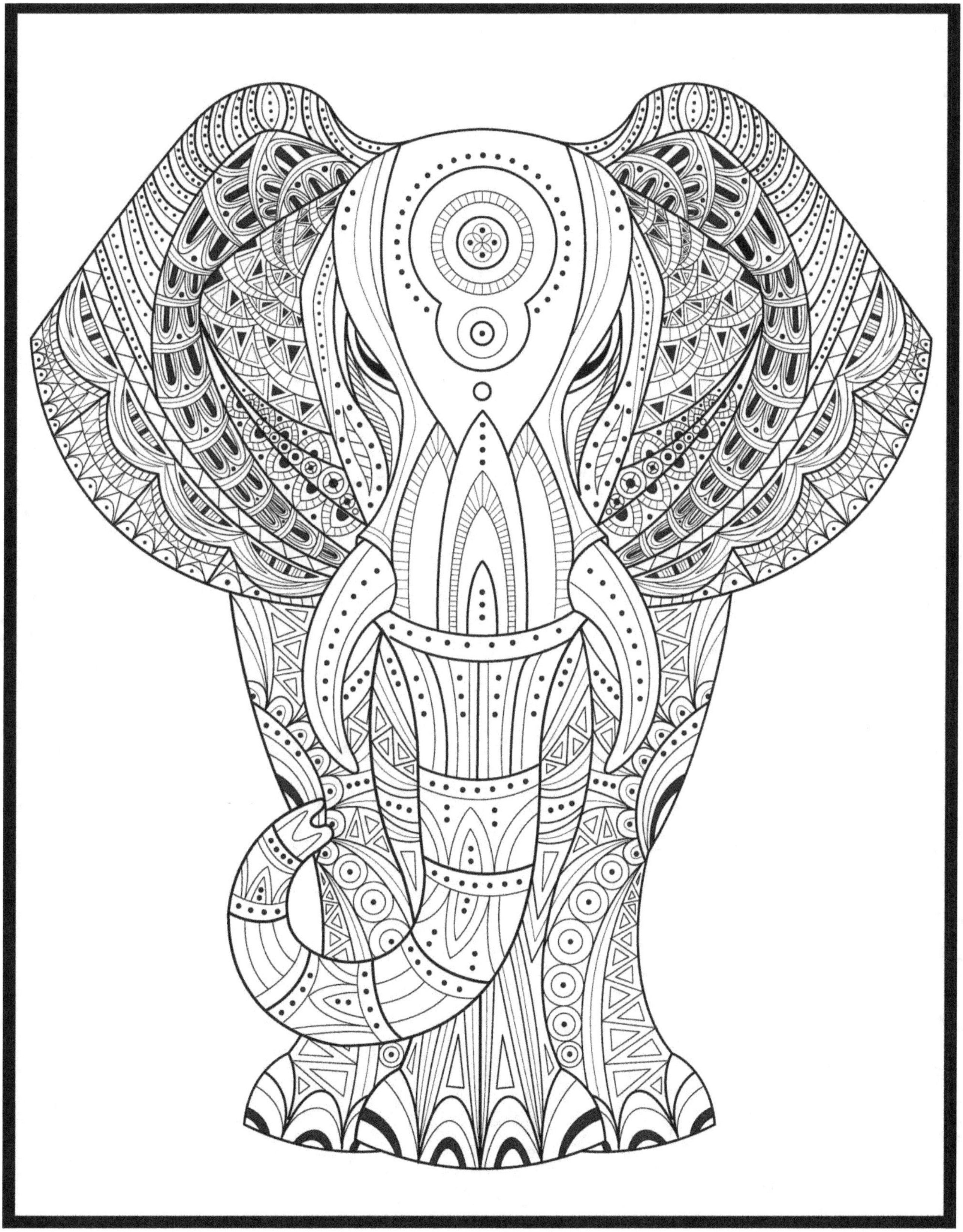

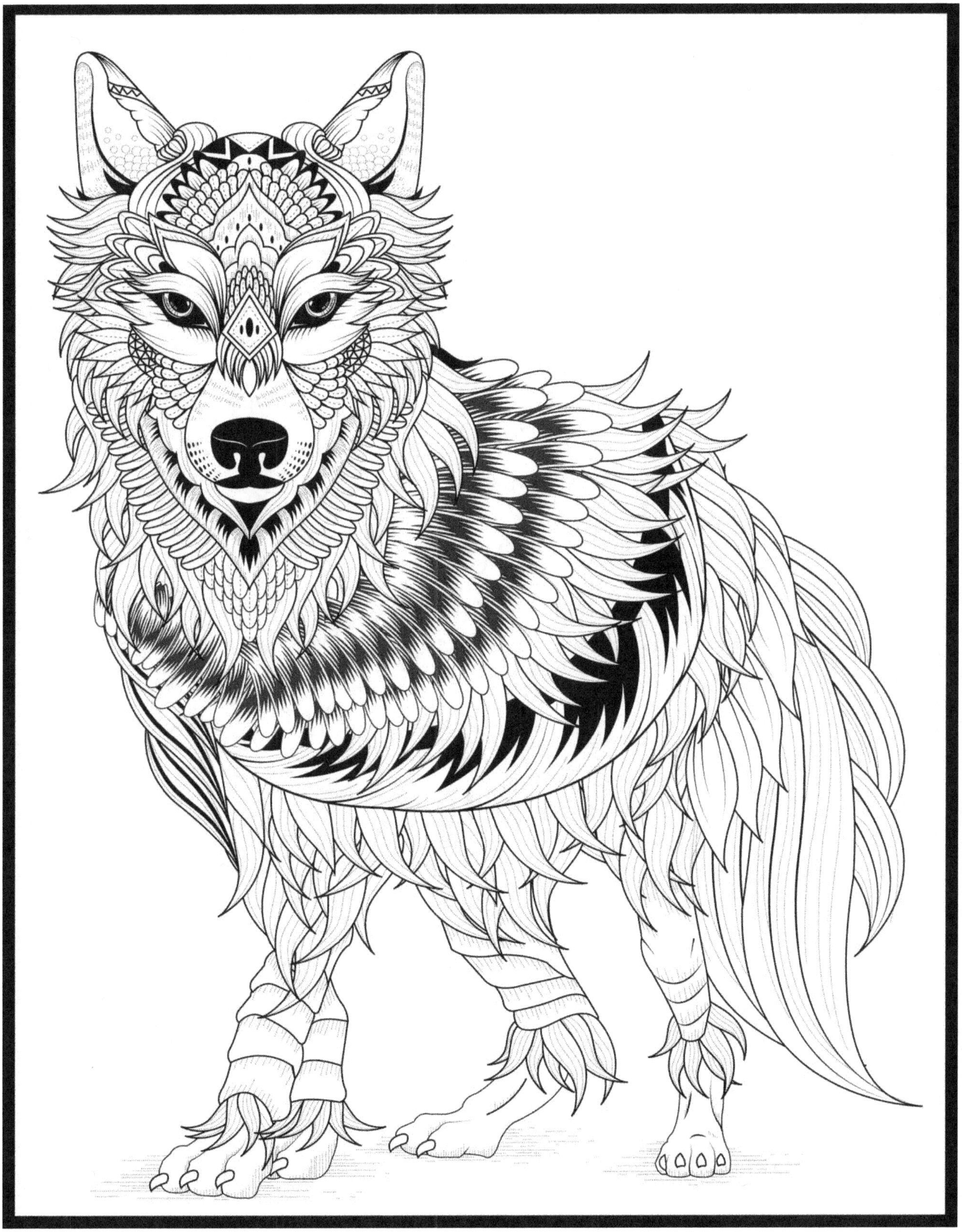

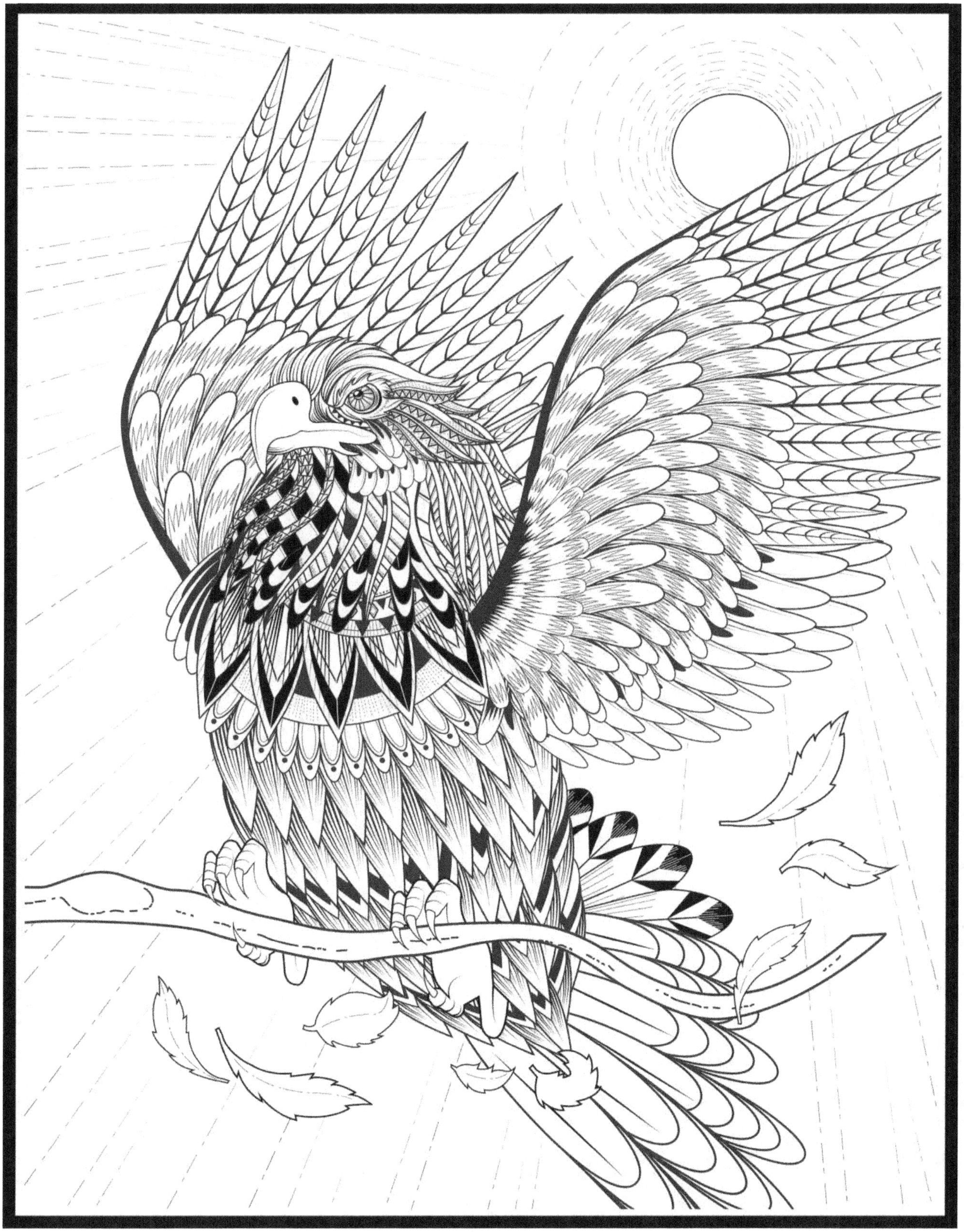

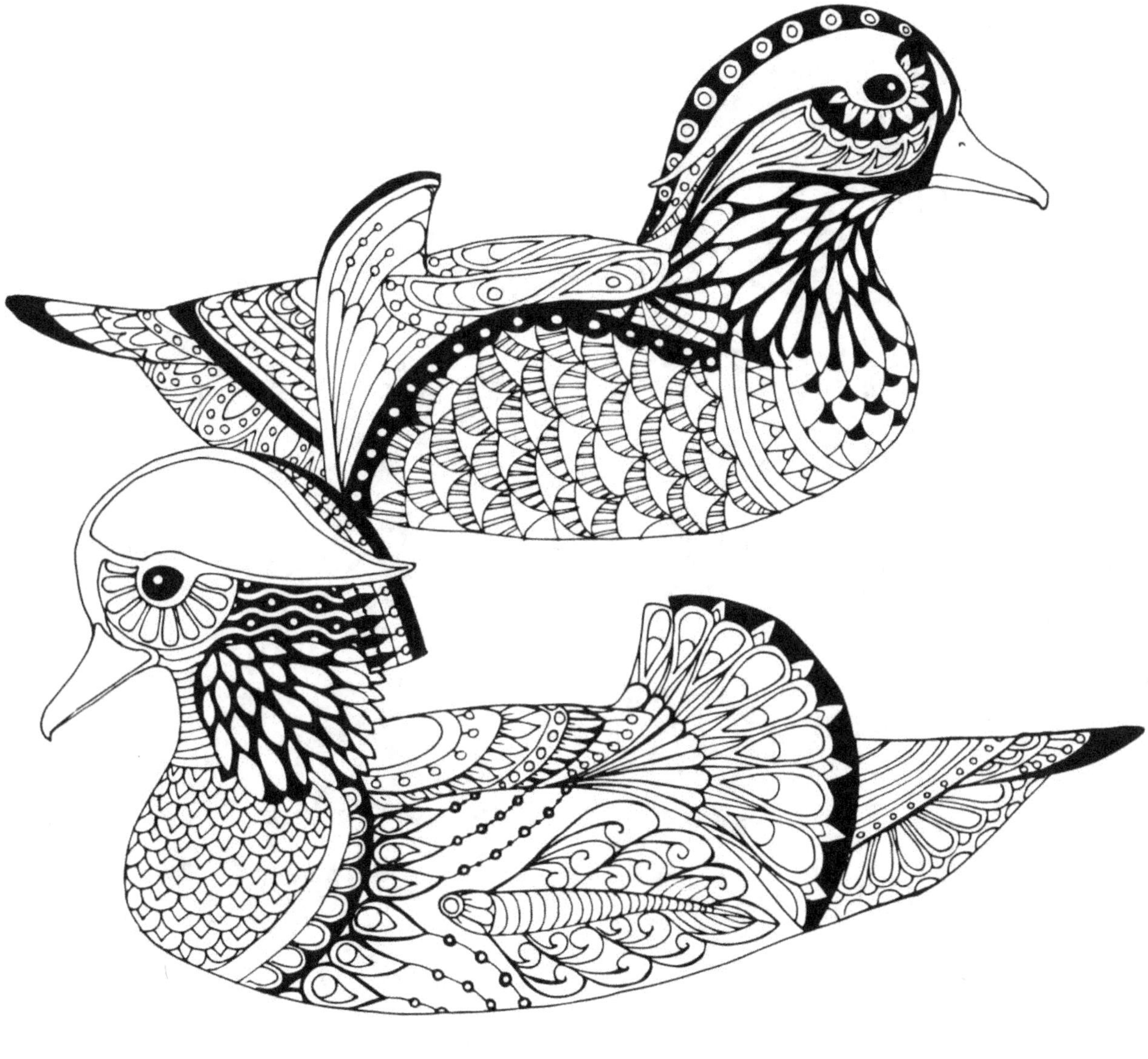

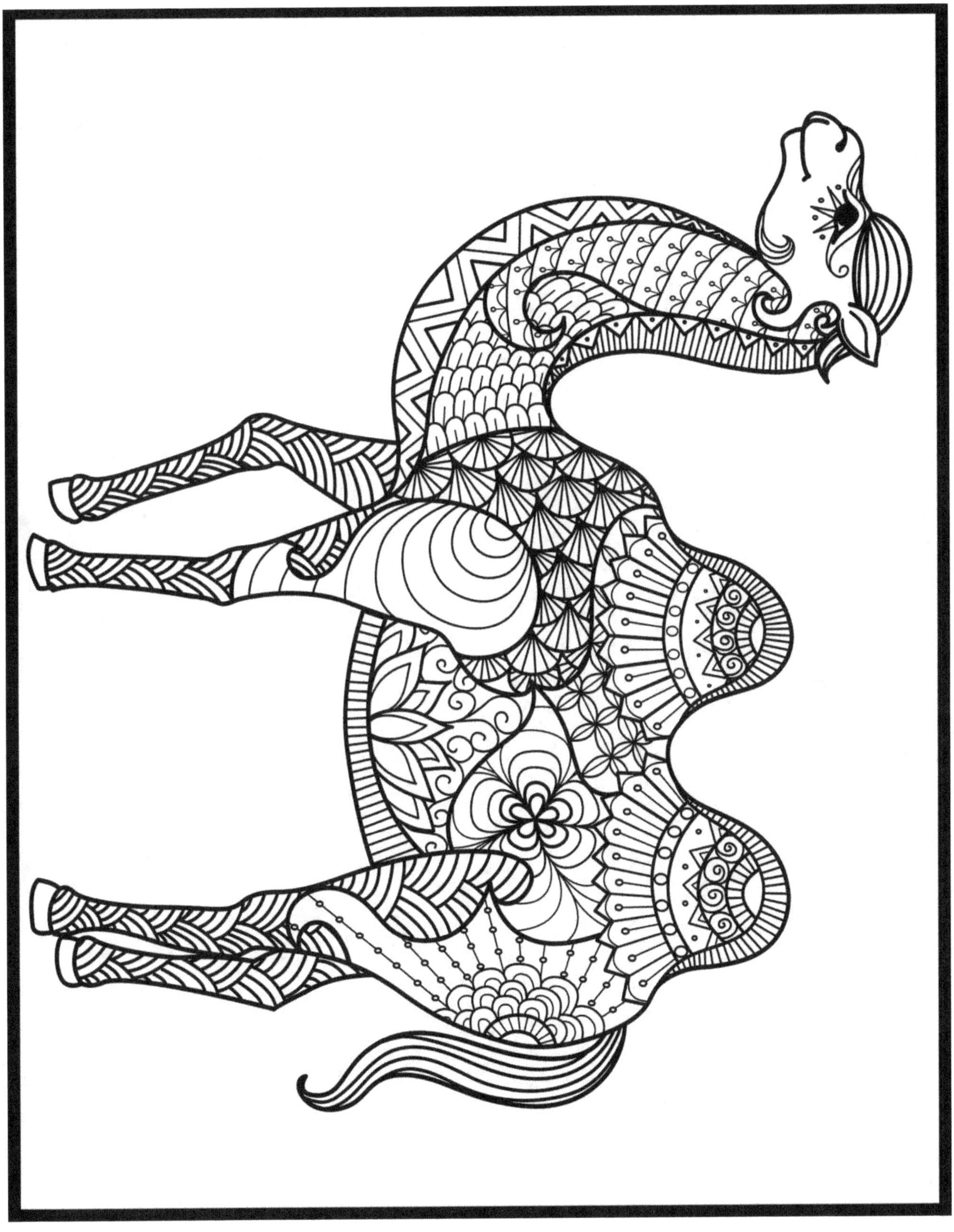

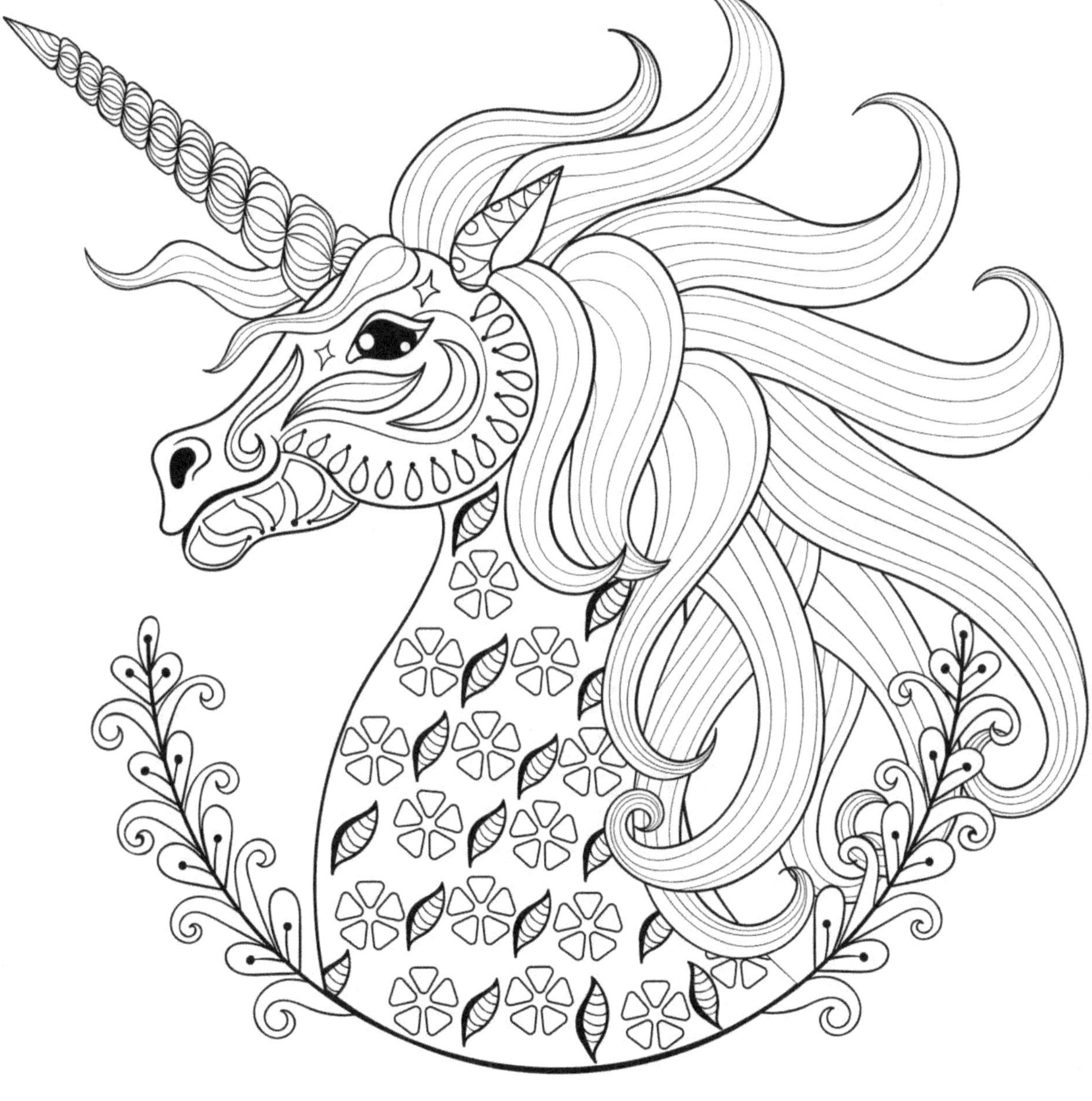

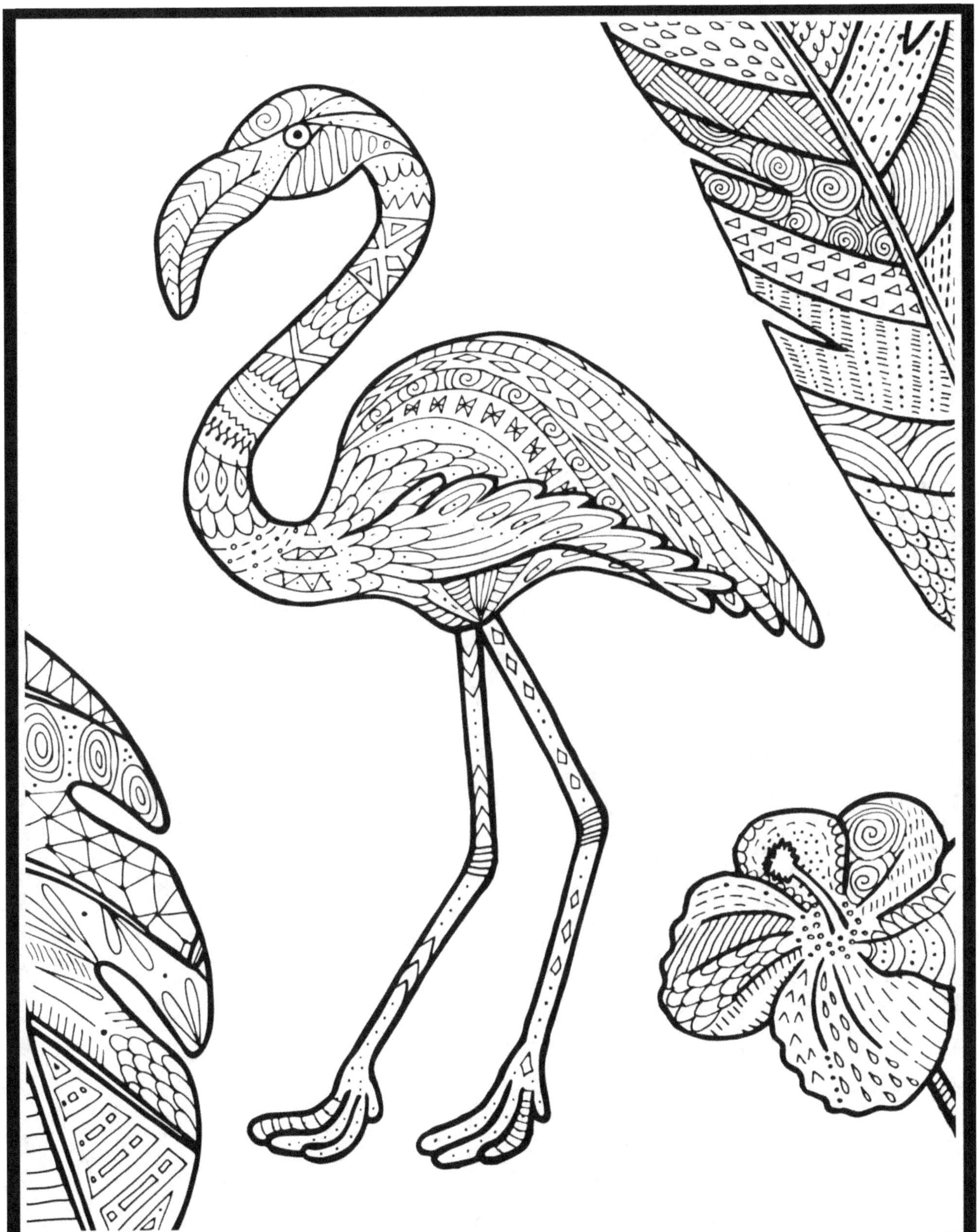

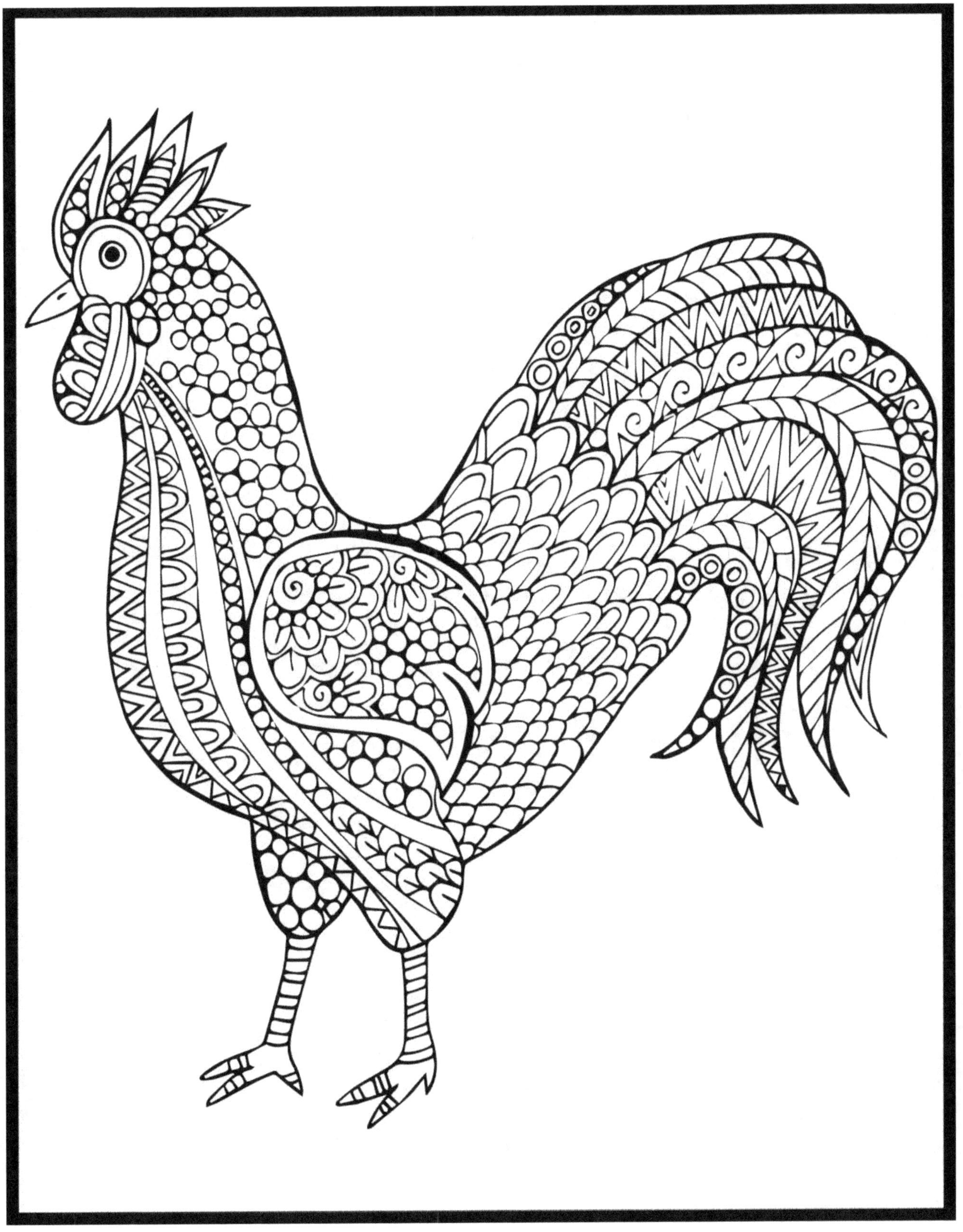

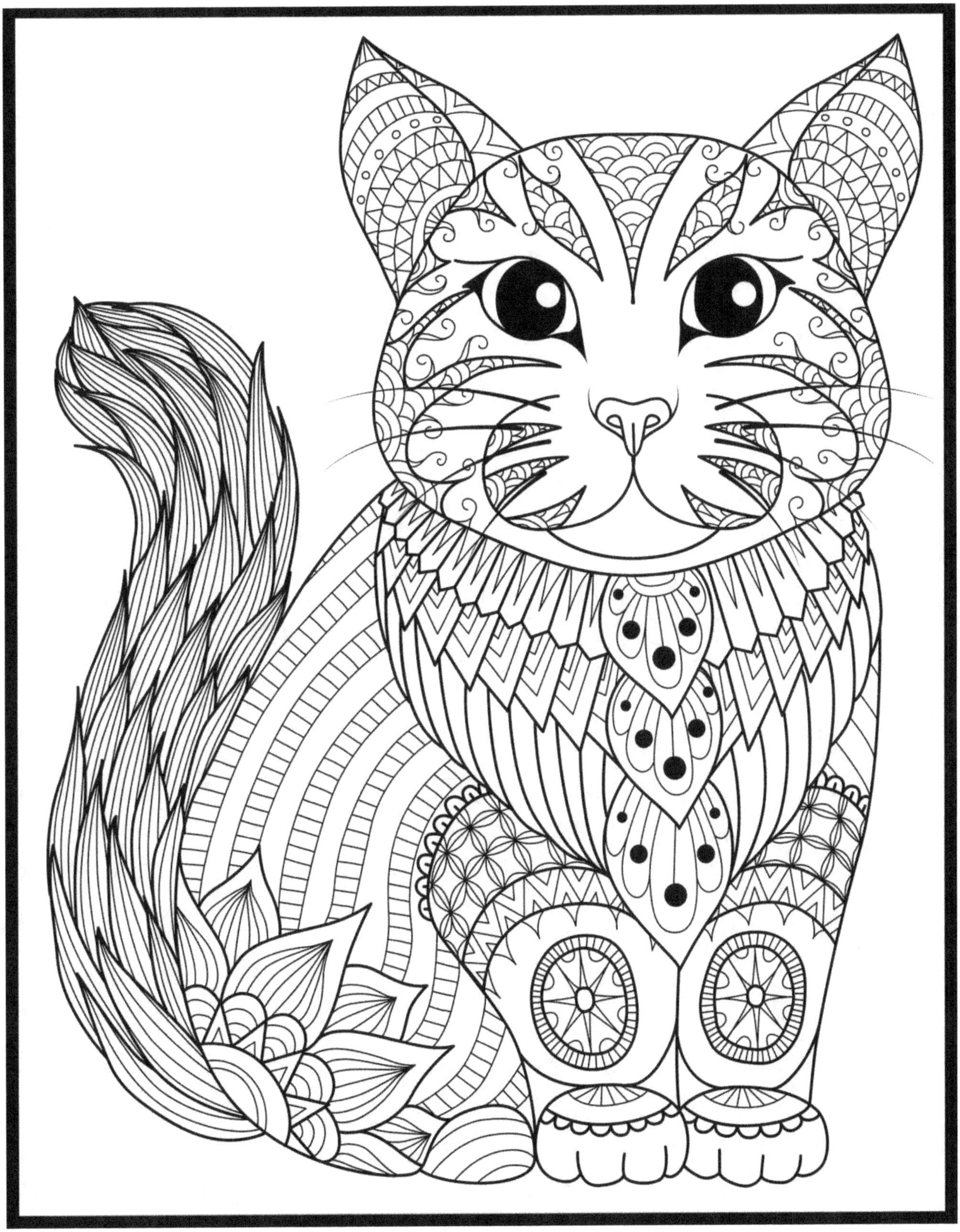

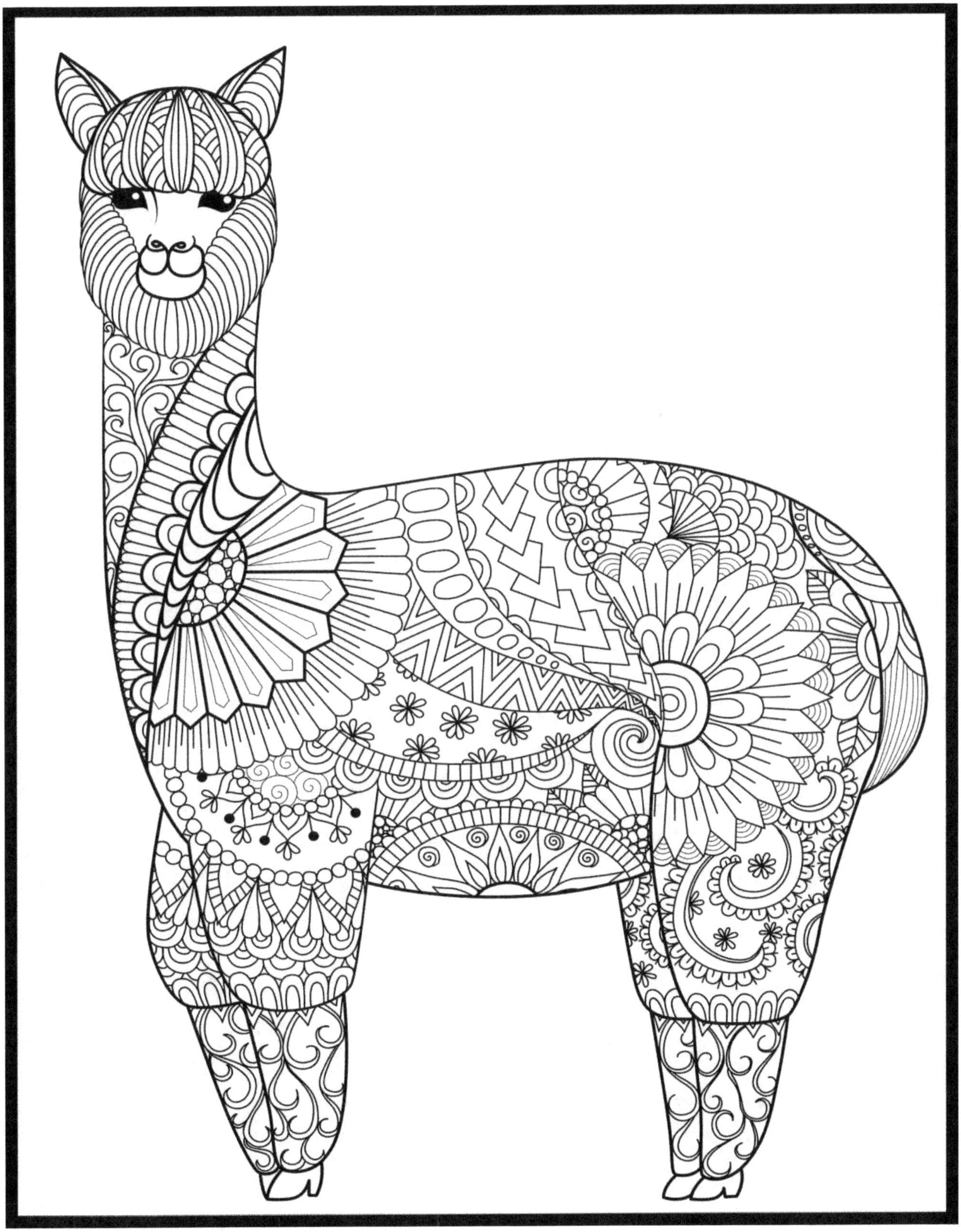

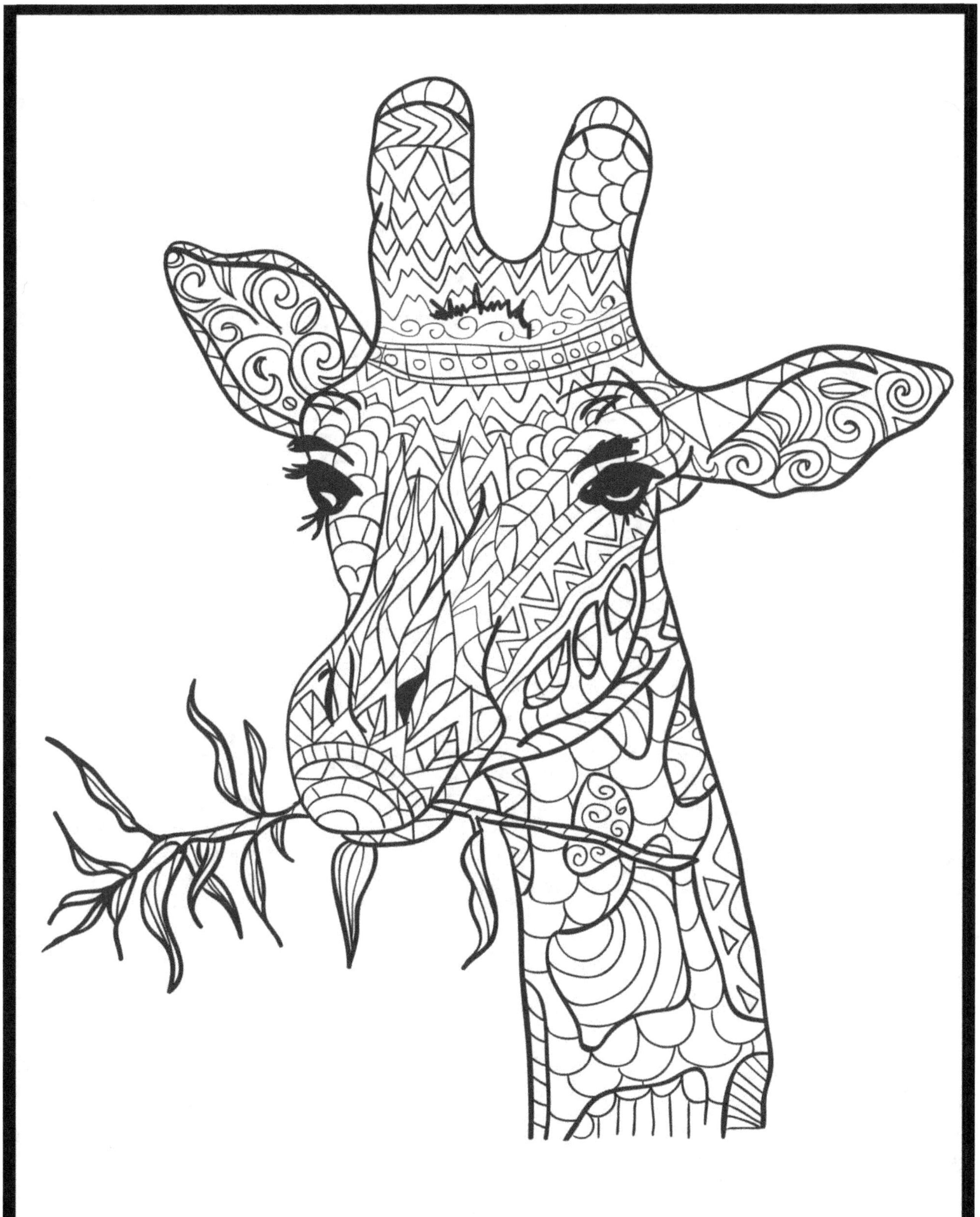

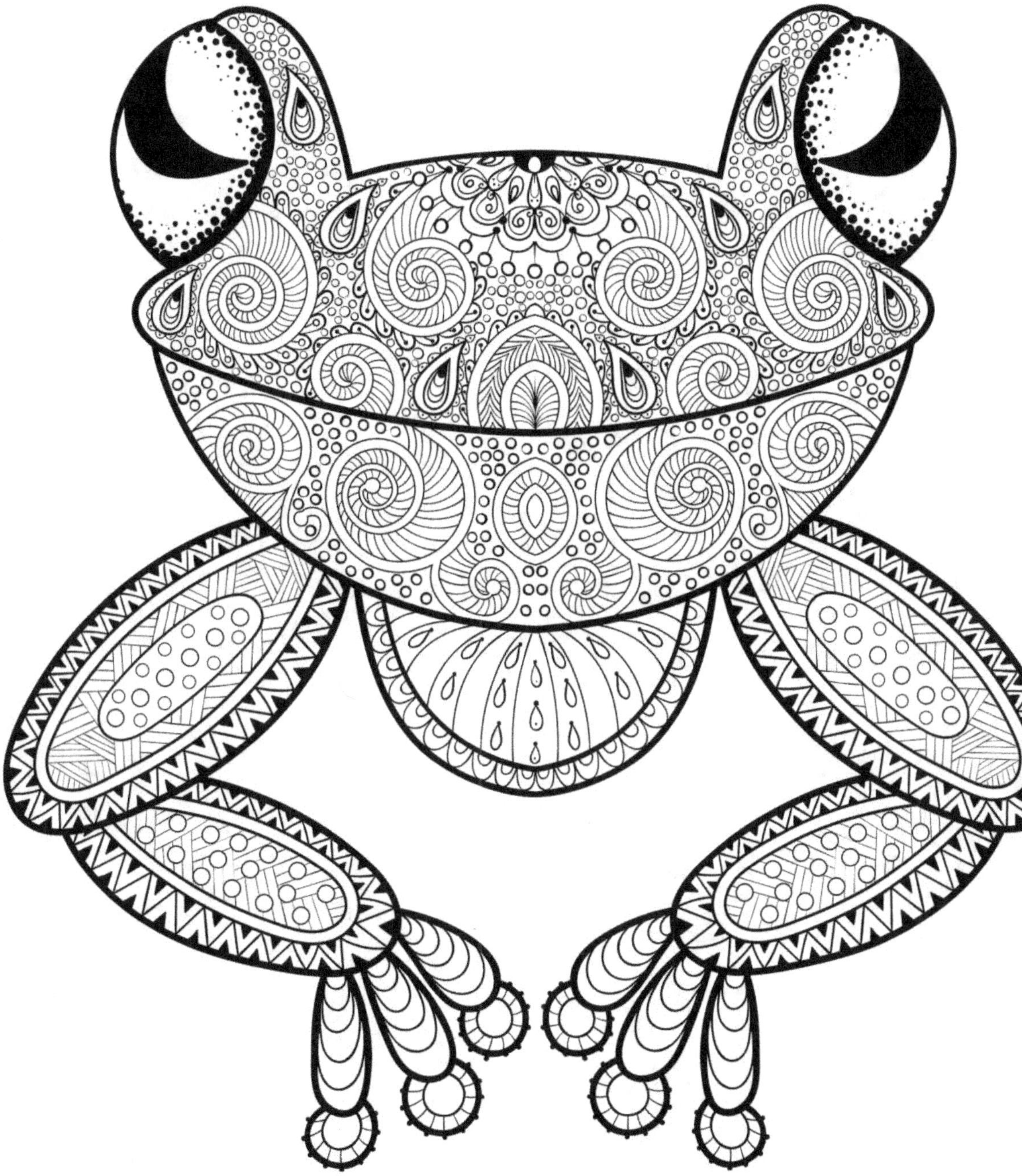

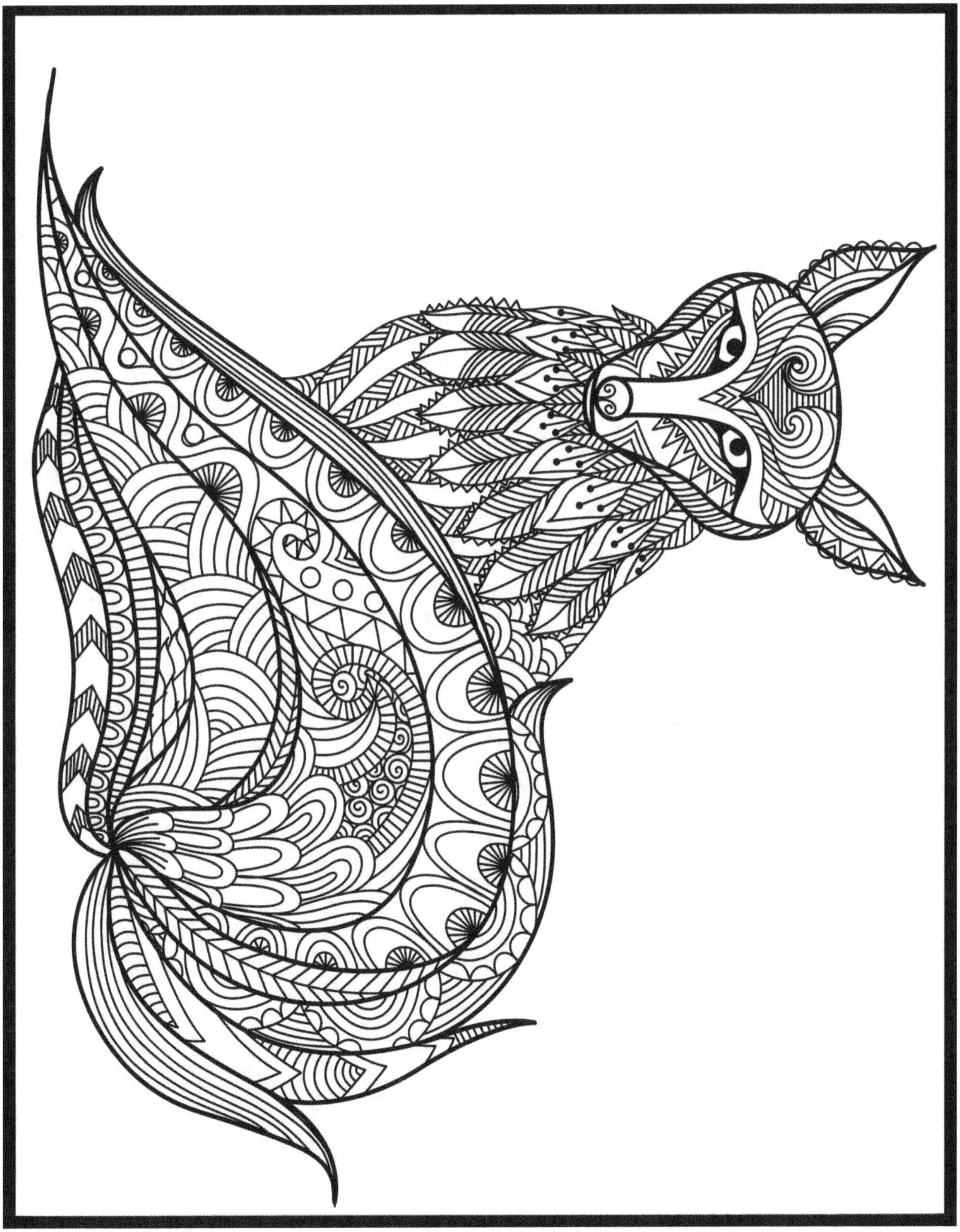

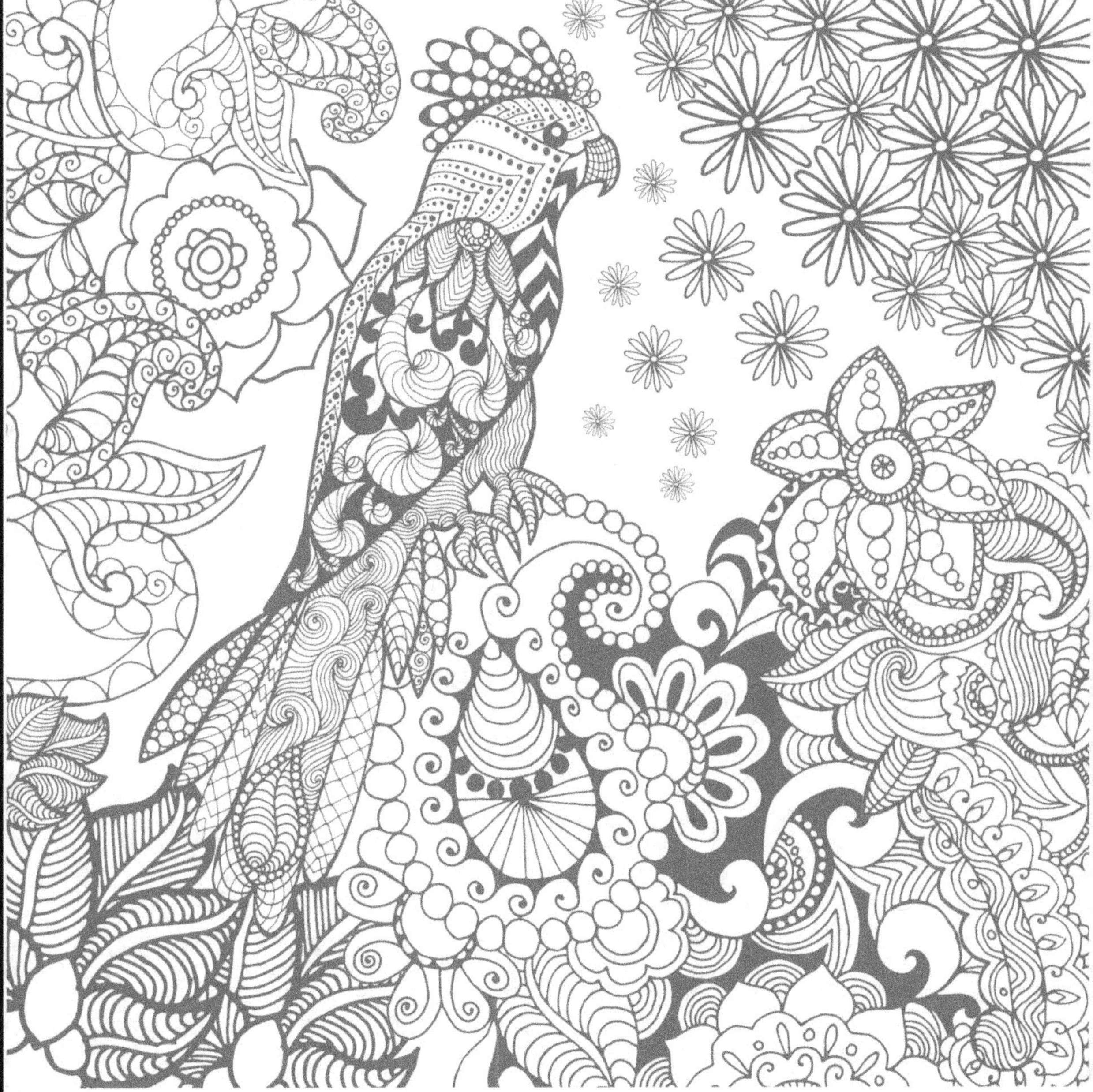

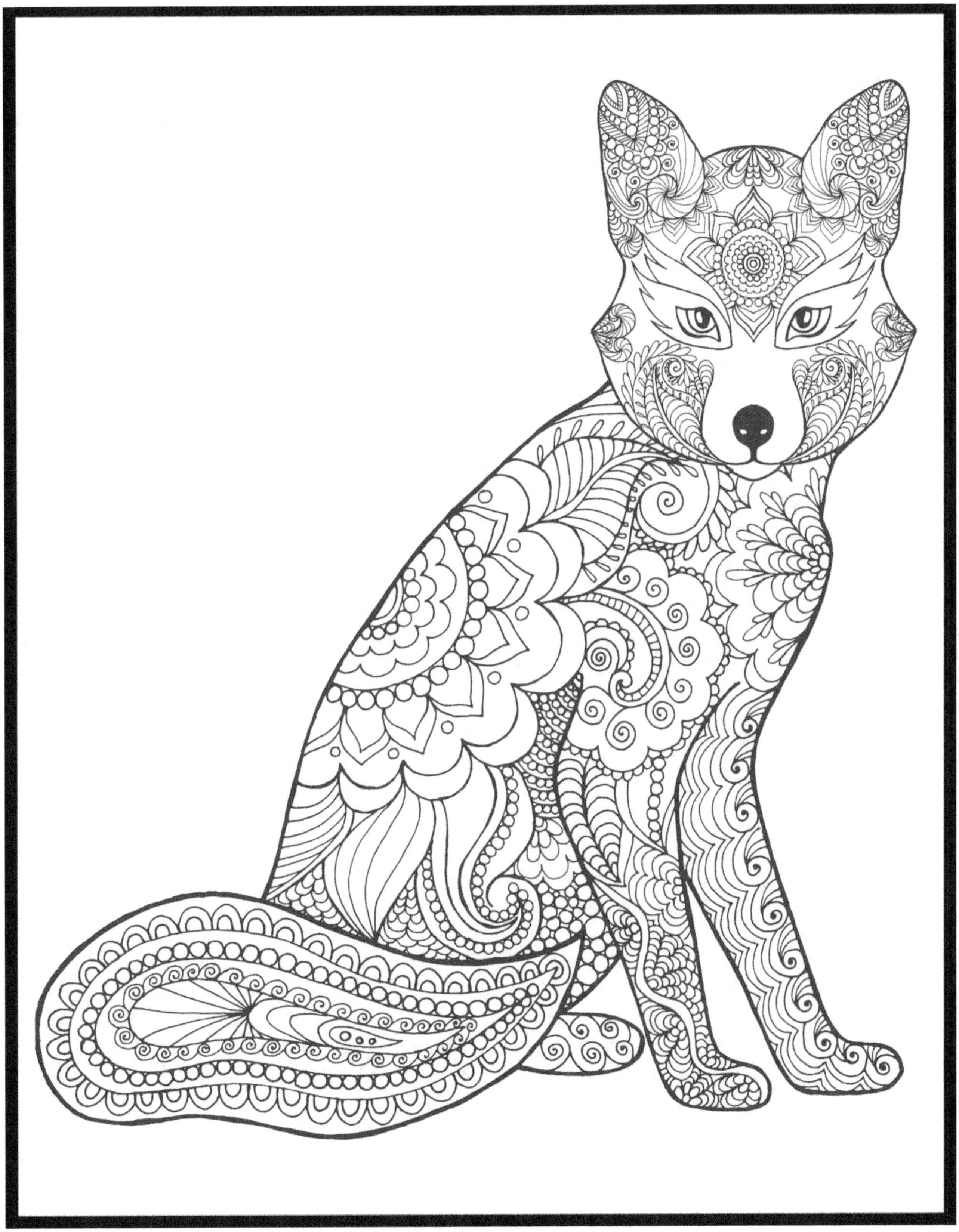

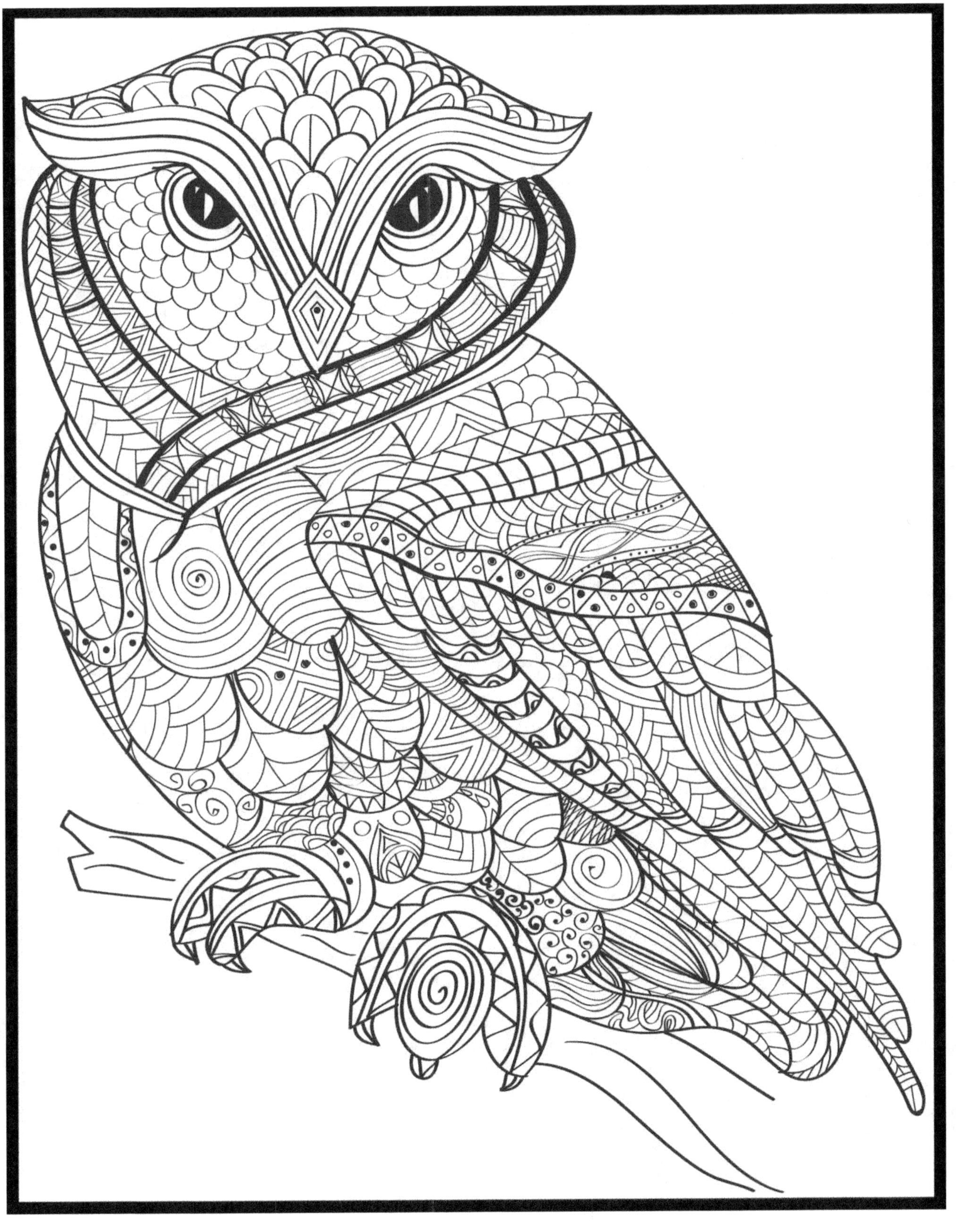

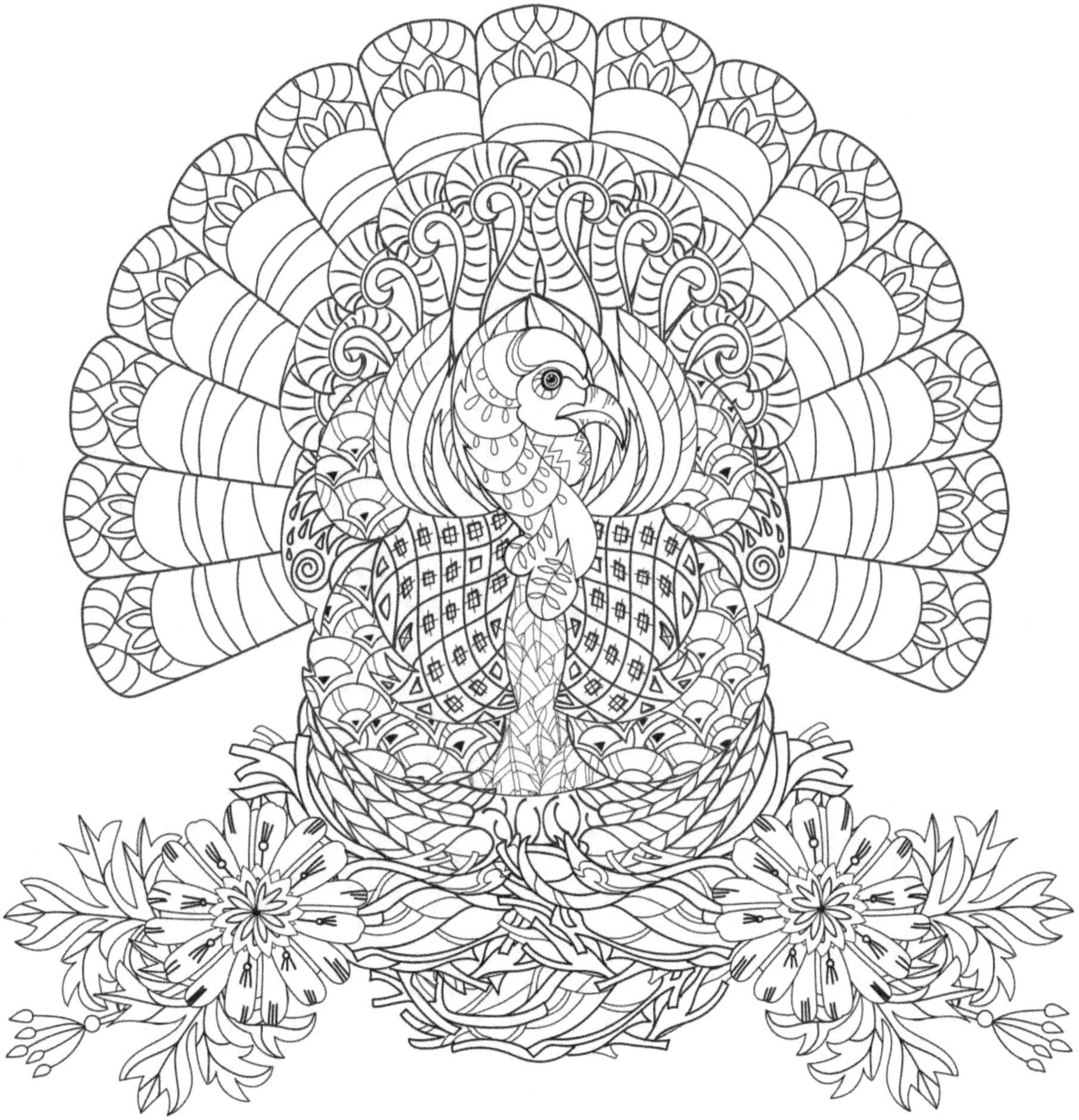

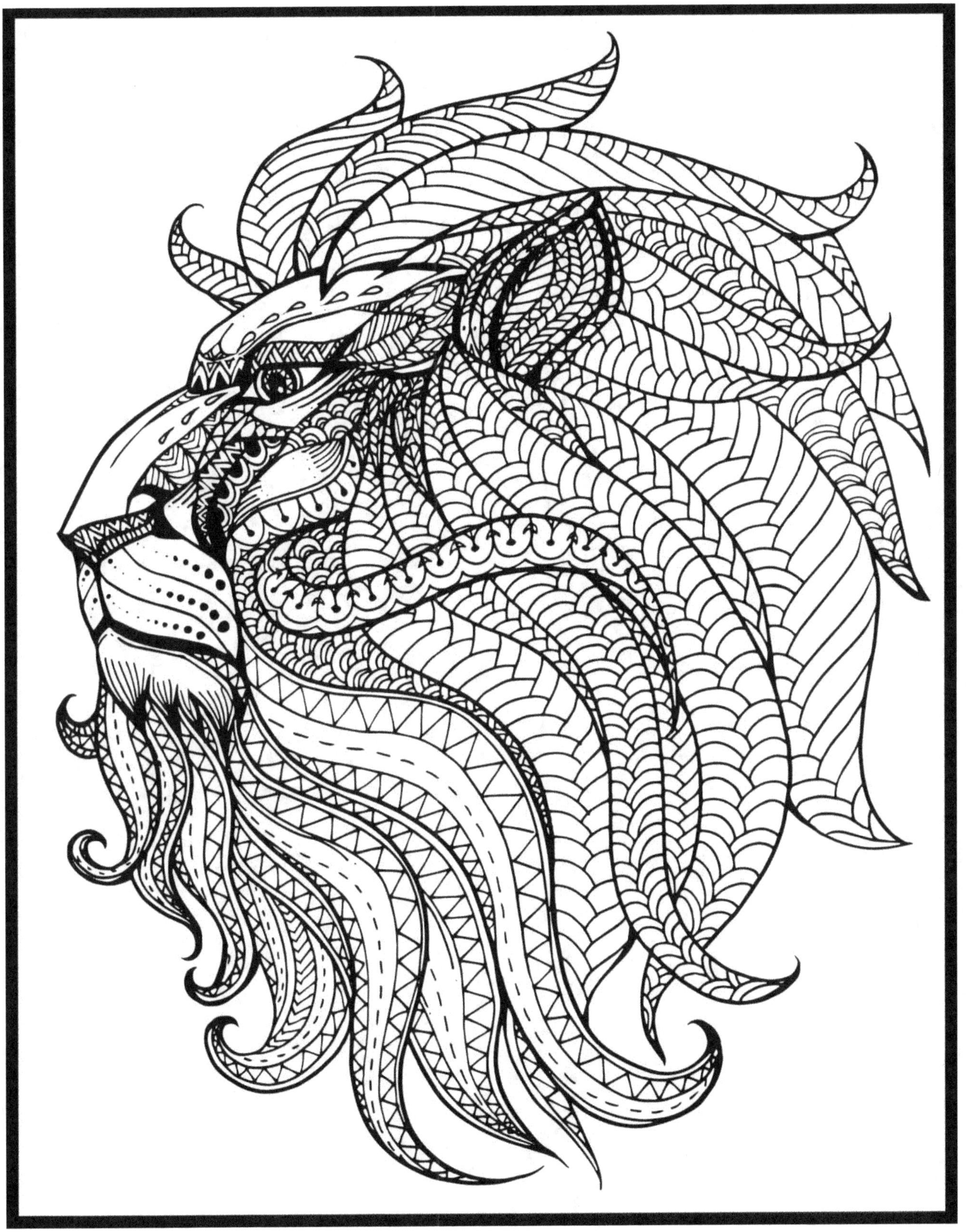

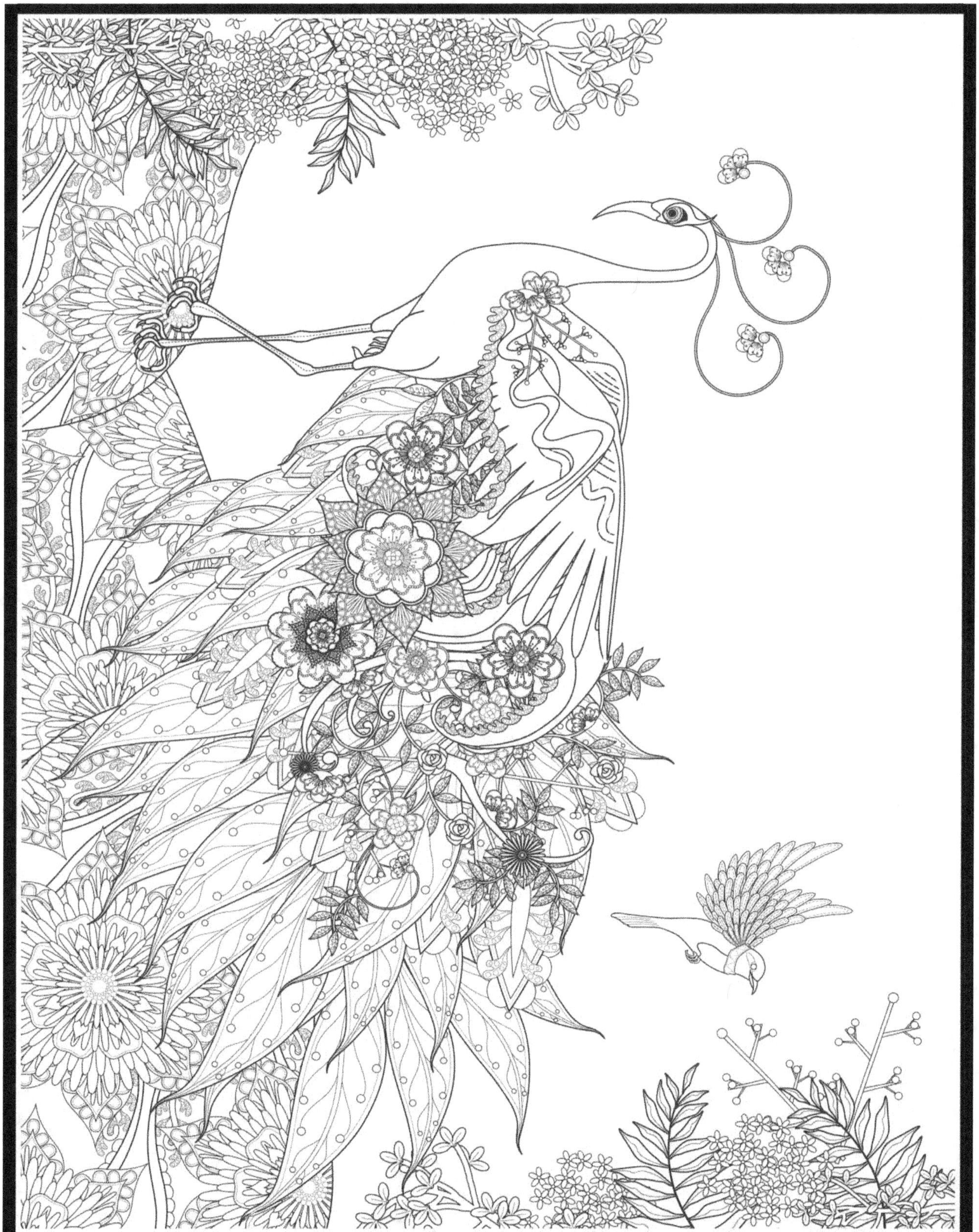

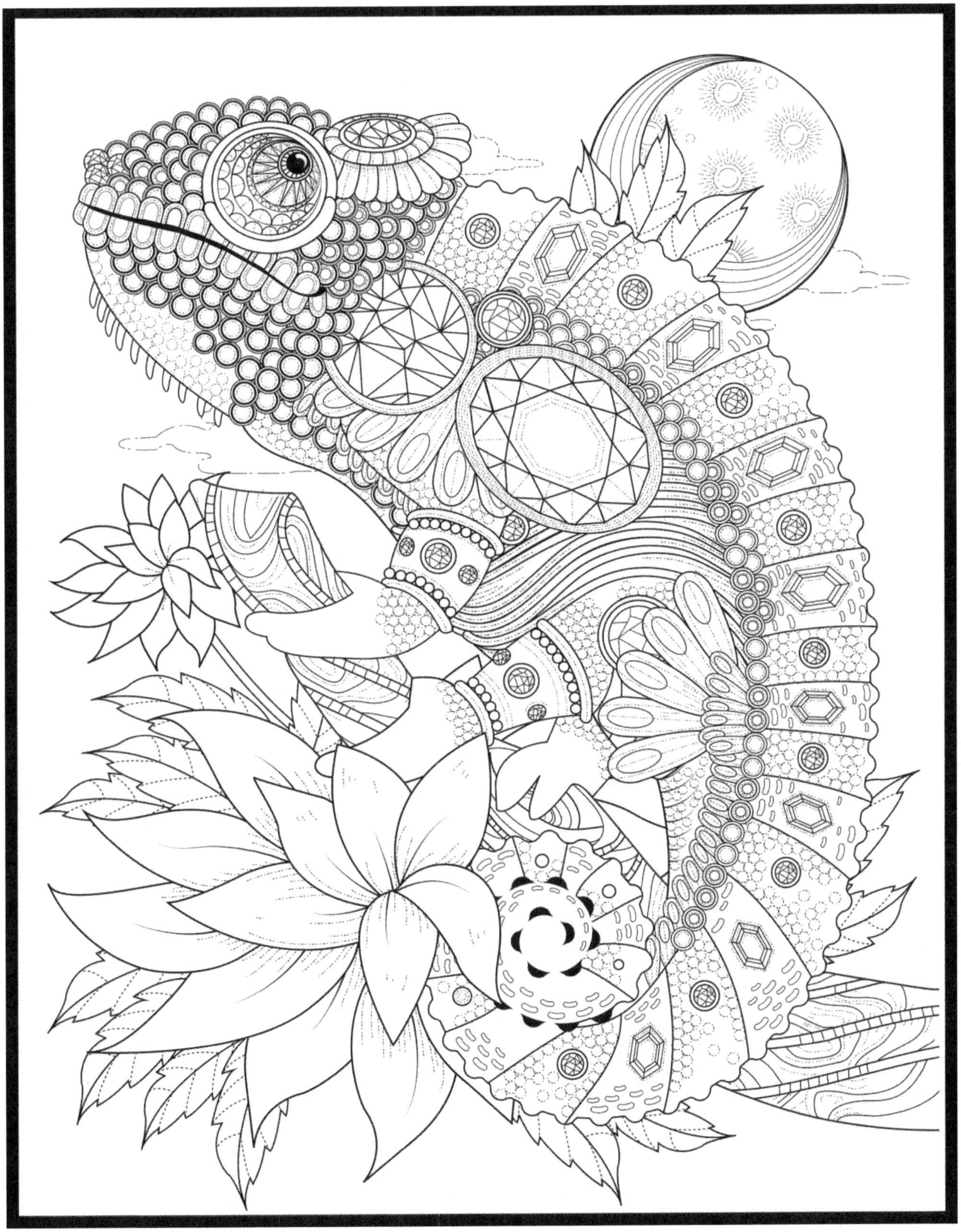

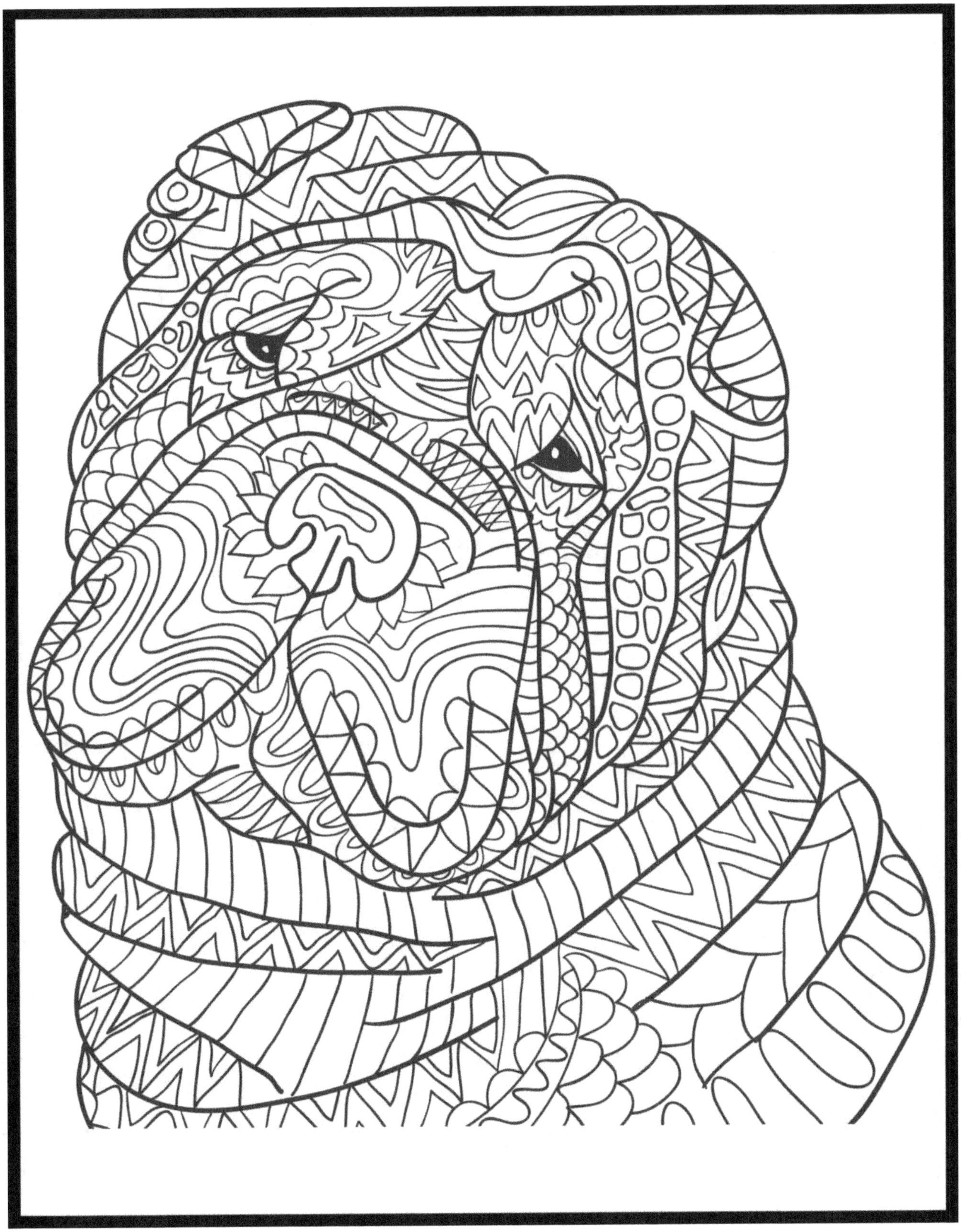

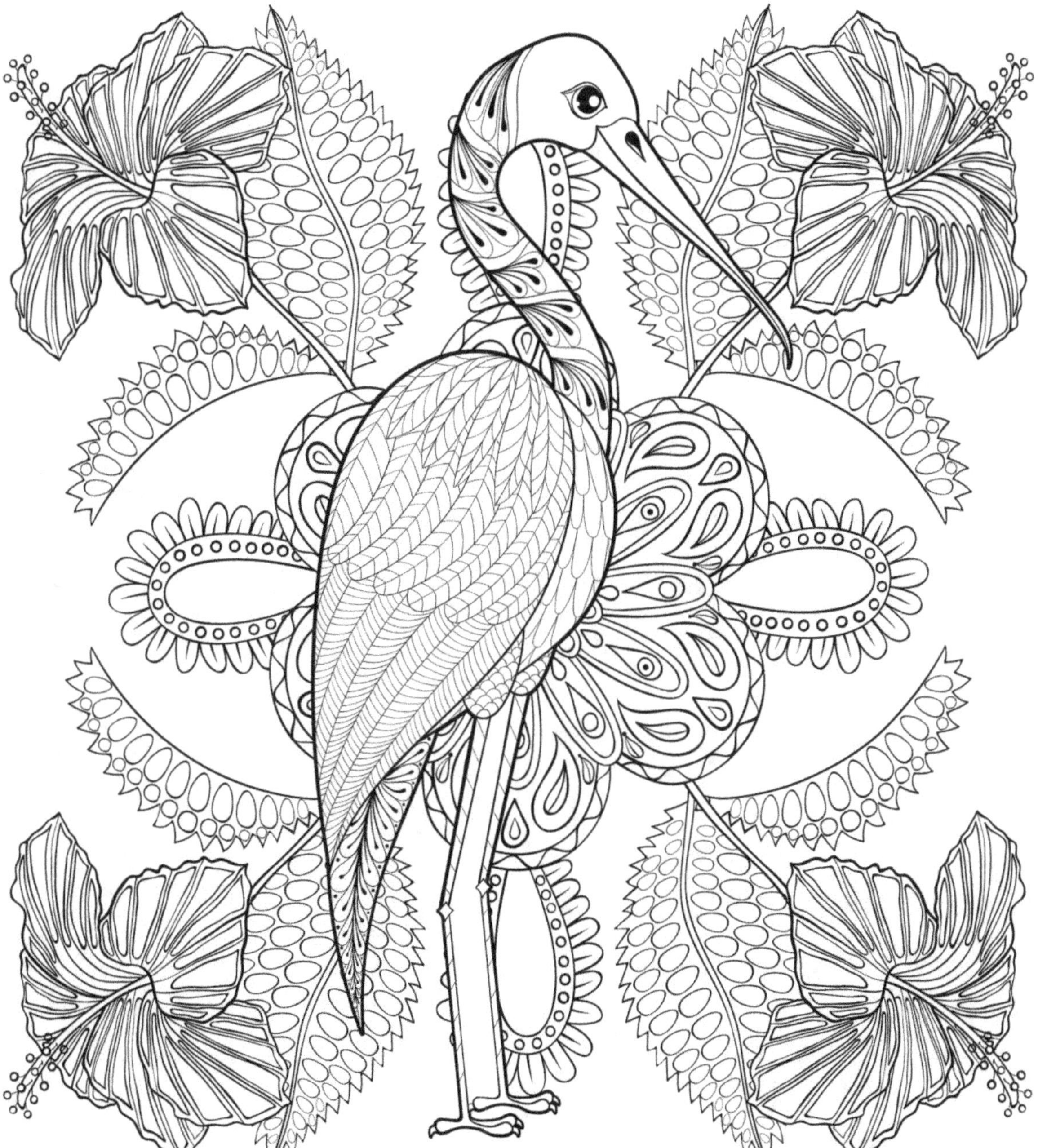

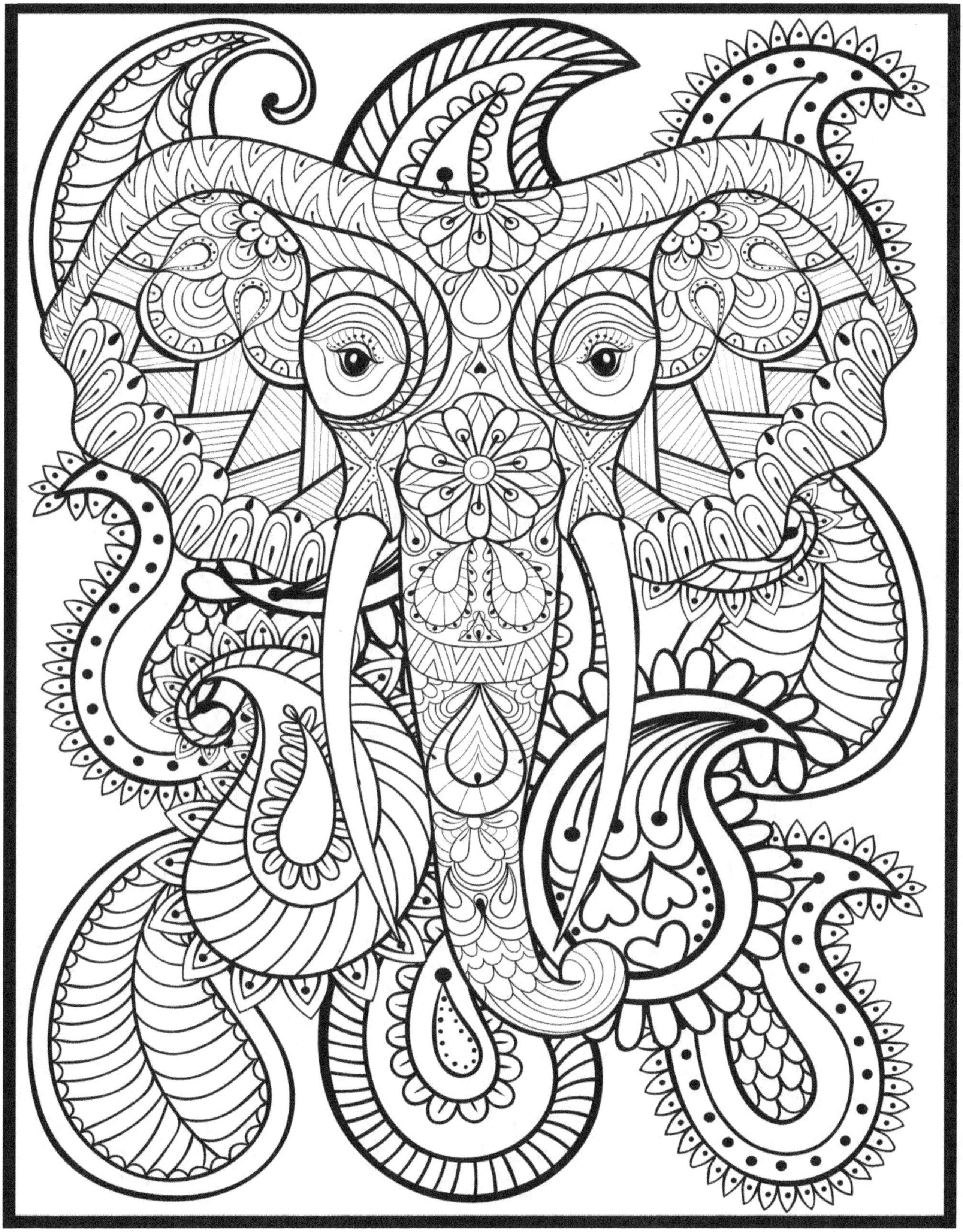

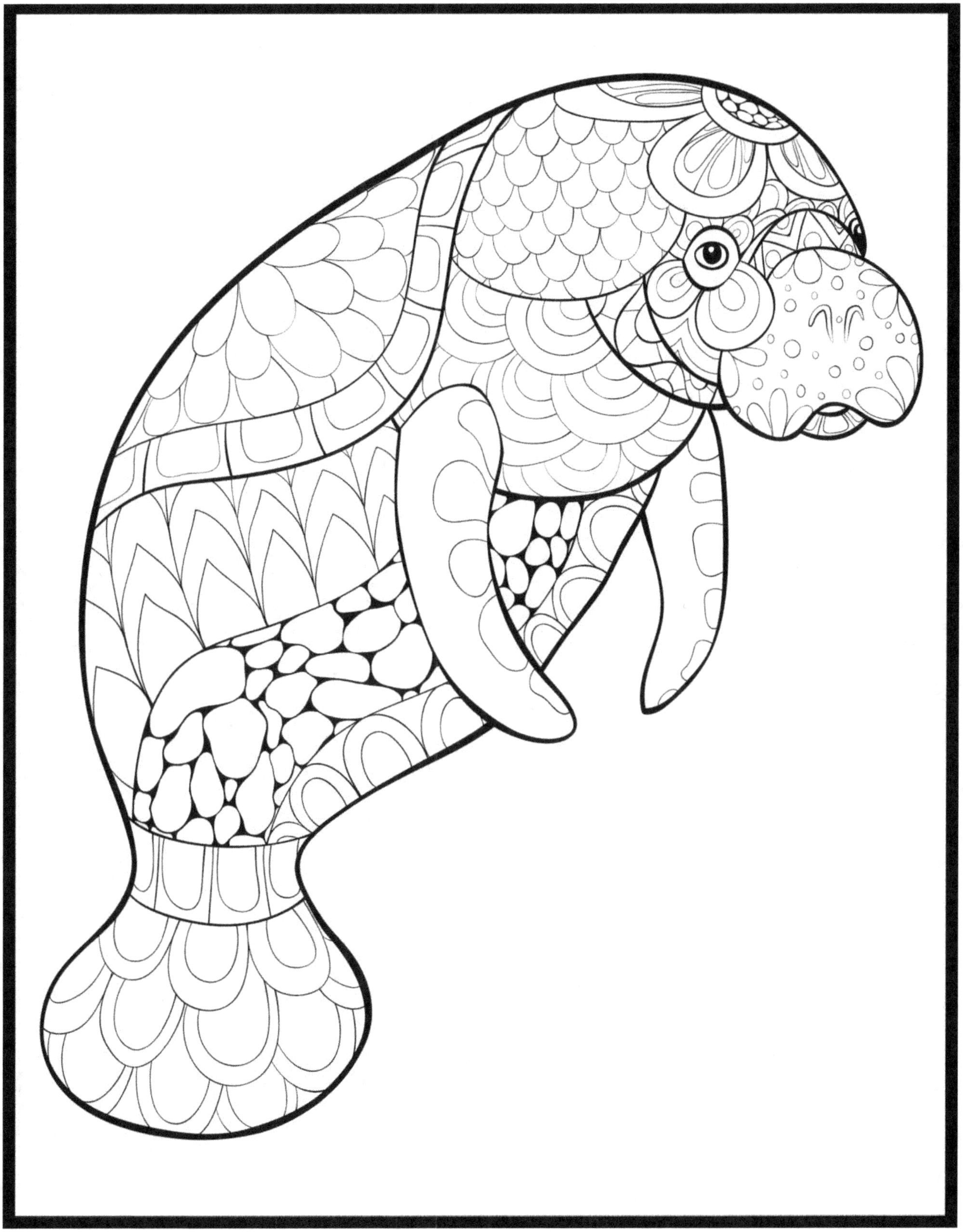

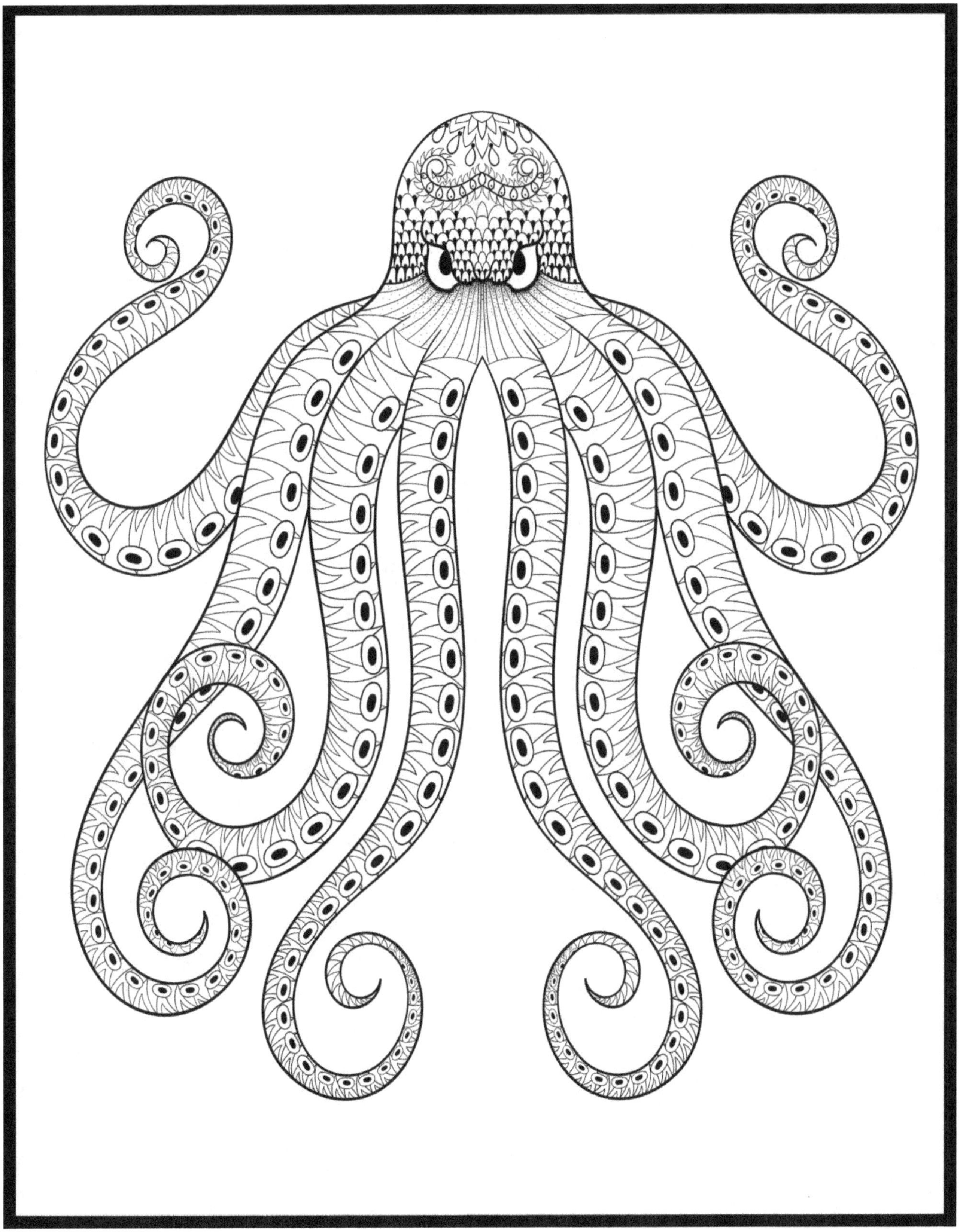

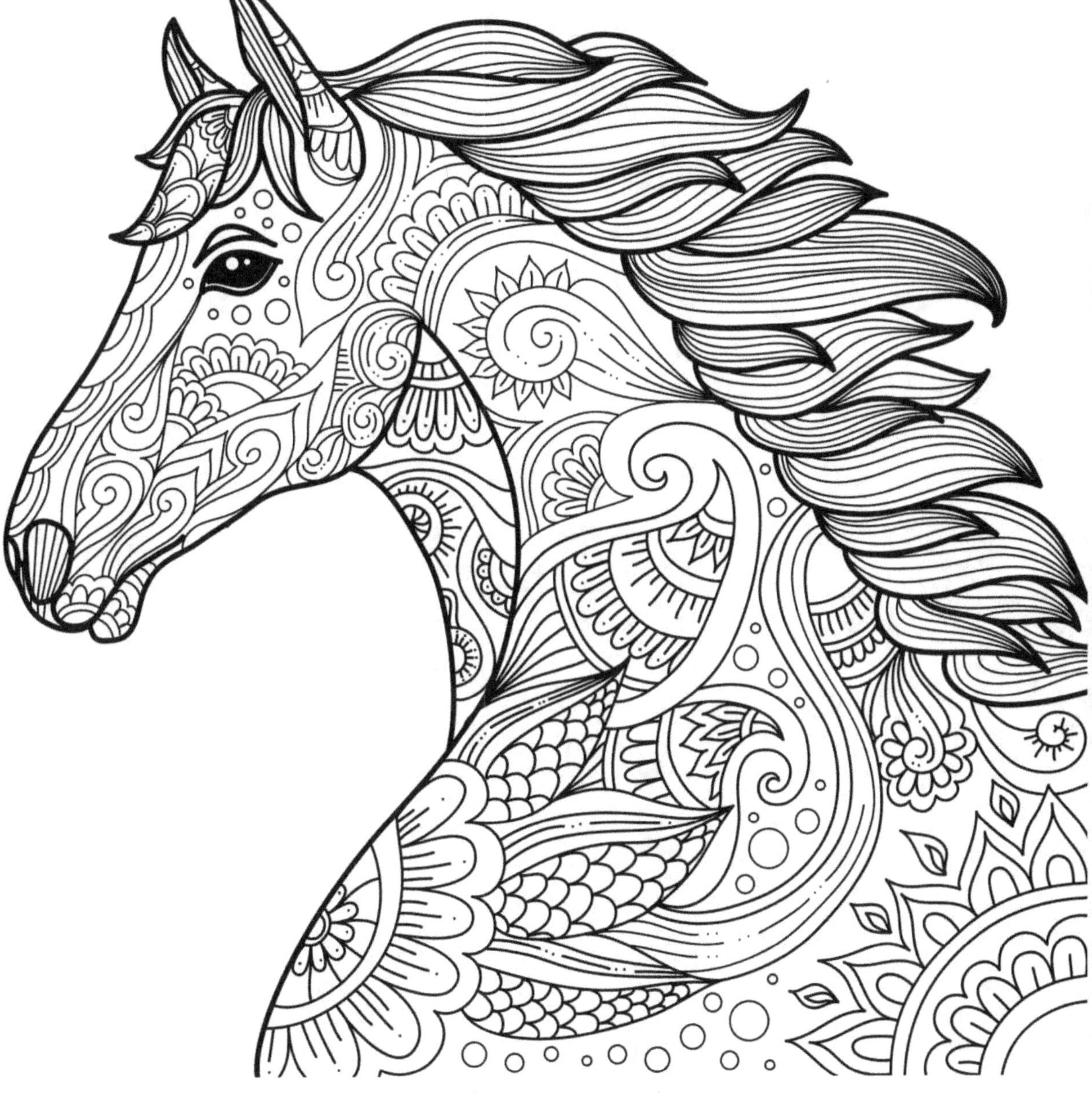

www.ingramcontent.com/pod-product-compliance
Lightning Source LLC
Chambersburg PA
CBHW082113220526
45472CB00009B/2163
* 9 7 8 1 7 2 0 4 5 8 7 0 8 *